The Constitution of
The State of Massachusetts:
A Quick Reference Guide

Bootblack Budget Books
Copyright 2018 ©
ISBN-13: 978-1986542593
ISBN-10: 1986542599

Contents:

Preamble – Page 8

Part The First: A Declaration of the Rights of the Inhabitants of the Commonwealth of Massachusetts

Article I – Page 9
Article II – Page 10
Article III – Page 11
Article IV – Page 13
Article V – Page 14
Article VI – Page 15
Article VII – Page 16
Article VIII – Page 17
Article IX – Page 18
Article X – Page 19
Article XI – Page 20
Article XII – Page 21
Article XIII – Page 22
Article XIV – Page 23
Article XV – Page 24
Article XVI – Page 25
Article XVII – Page 26
Article XVIII – Page 27
Article XIX – Page 28
Article XX – Page 29
Article XXI – Page 30
Article XXII – Page 31
Article XXIII – Page 32
Article XXIV – Page 33
Article XXV – Page 34
Article XXVI – Page 35
Article XXVII – Page 36
Article XXVIII – Page 37
Article XXIX – Page 38
Article XXX – Page 39

Part The Second: The Frame of Government

Frame of Government – Page 40

Chapter I: The Legislative Power

Section I. The General Court:

Article I – Page 41
Article II – Page 42
Article III – Page 43
Article IV – Page 44

Section II. The Senate:

Article I – Page 47
Article II – Page 48
Article III– Page 50
Article IV– Page 51
Article V – Page 52
Article VI– Page 53
Article VII– Page 54
Article VIII– Page 55
Article IX – Page 56

Section III. House Of Representatives:

Article I – Page 57
Article II – Page 58
Article III– Page 59
Article IV– Page 60
Article V – Page 61
Article VI– Page 62
Article VII– Page 63
Article VIII– Page 64
Article IX – Page 65
Article X – Page 66
Article XI – Page 67

Chapter II: Executive Power

Section I. The Governor:

Article I – Page 68
Article II – Page 69
Article III– Page 70
Article IV– Page 71
Article V – Page 72
Article VI– Page 73
Article VII– Page 74
Article VIII– Page 76

Article IX – Page 77
Article X – Page 78
Article XI – Page 80
Article XII – Page 81
Article XIII – Page 82

Section II. Lieutenant-Governor:

Article I – Page 83
Article II – Page 84
Article III – Page 85

Section III. Council, And The Manner Of Settling Elections By The Legislature:

Article I – Page 86
Article II – Page 87
Article III – Page 88
Article IV – Page 89
Article V – Page 90
Article VI – Page 91
Article VII – Page 92

Section IV: Secretary, Treasurer, Commissary, Etc:

Article I – Page 93
Article II – Page 94

Chapter III: Judiciary Power:

Article I – Page 95
Article II – Page 96
Article III – Page 97
Article IV – Page 99
Article V – Page 100

Chapter IV: Delegates To Congress – Page 100

Chapter V: The University At Cambridge, And Encouragement Of Literature, Etc:

Section I. The University

Article I – Page 101
Article II – Page 102
Article III – Page 103

Section II. The Encouragement Of Literature, Etc. – Page 104

Chapter VI: Oaths And Subscriptions; Incompatibility Of And Exclusion From Offices; Pecuniary Qualifications; Commissions; Writs; Confirmation Of Laws; Habeas Corpus; The Enacting Style; Continuance Of Officers; Provision For A Future Revisal Of The Constitution, Etc.

Article I – Page 105
Article II – Page 108
Article III– Page 110
Article IV– Page 111
Article V – Page 112
Article VI– Page 113
Article VII– Page 114
Article VIII– Page 115
Article IX – Page 116
Article X – Page 117
Article XI – Page 118

ARTICLES OF AMENDMENT:

Article I – Page 119
Article II – Page 120
Article III – Page 121
Article IV – Page 122
Article V – Page 123
Article VI – Page 124
Article VII – Page 125
Article VIII – Page 126
Article IX – Page 127
Article X – Page 128
Article XI – Page 130
Article XII – Page 131
Article XIII – Page 133
Article XIV – Page 136
Article XV – Page 137
Article XVI – Page 138
Article XVII – Page 140
Article XVIII – Page 141
Article XIX – Page 142
Article XX – Page 143
Article XXI – Page 144
Article XXII – Page 146
Article XXIII – Page 147
Article XXIV – Page 148
Article XXV – Page 149
Article XXVI – Page 150
Article XXVII – Page 151
Article XXVIII – Page 152
Article XXIX – Page 153
Article XXX – Page 154
Article XXXI – Page 155
Article XXXII – Page 156
Article XXXIII – Page 157
Article XXXIV – Page 158
Article XXXV – Page 159
Article XXXVI – Page 160

Article XXXVII – Page 161
Article XXXVIII – Page 162
Article XXXIX – Page 163
Article XL – Page 164
Article XLI – Page 165
Article XLII – Page 166
Article XLIII – Page 167
Article XLIV – Page 168
Article XLV – Page 169
Article XLVI – Page 170
Article XVIII – Page 171
Article XLVII – Page 173
Article XLVIII – Page 174
Article XLIX – Page 189
Article L – Page 190
Article LI – Page 191
Article LII – Page 192
Article LIII – Page 193
Article LIV – Page 194
Article LV – Page 195
Article LVI – Page 196
Article LVII – Page 197
Article LVIII – Page 198
Article LIX – Page 199
Article LX – Page 200
Article LXI – Page 201
Article LXII – Page 202
Article LXIII – Page 203
Article LXIV – Page 205
Article LXV – Page 206
Article LXVI – Page 207
Article LXVII – Page 208
Article LXVIII – Page 209
Article LXIX – Page 210
Article LXX – Page 211
Article LXXI – Page 212

Article LXXII – Page 215
Article LXXIII – Page 216
Article LXXIV – Page 217
Article LXXV – Page 220
Article LXXVI – Page 221
Article LXXVII – Page 222
Article LXXVIII – Page 223
Article LXXIX – Page 224
Article LXXX – Page 225
Article LXXXII – Page 231
Article LXXXIII – Page 233
Article LXXXIV – Page 234
Article LXXXV – Page 235
Article LXXXVI – Page 236
Article LXXXVII – Page 237
Article LXXXVIII – Page 239
Article LXXXIX – Page 240
Article XC – Page 246
Article XCI – Page 248
Article XCII – Page 250
Article XCIII – Page 252
Article XCIV – Page 253
Article XCV – Page 254
Article XCVI – Page 255

Article XCVII – Page 256
Article XCVIII – Page 257
Article XCIX – Page 258
Article C – Page 259
Article CI – Page 260
Article CII – Page 262
Article CIII – Page 263
Article CIV – Page 264
Article CV – Page 265
Article CVI – Page 266
Article CVII – Page 267
Article CVIII – Page 268
Article CIX – Page 269
Article CX – Page 270
Article CXI – Page 271
Article CXII – Page 272
Article CXIII – Page 273
Article CXIV – Page 274
Article CXV – Page 275
Article CXVI – Page 276
Article CXVII – Page 277
Article CXVIII – Page 278
Article CXIX – Page 279
Article CXX – Page 280

PREAMBLE

The end of the institution, maintenance, and administration of government, is to secure the existence of the body politic, to protect it, and to furnish the individuals who compose it with the power of enjoying in safety and tranquility their natural rights, and the blessings of life: and whenever these great objects are not obtained, the people have a right to alter the government, and to take measures necessary for their safety, prosperity and happiness.

The body politic is formed by a voluntary association of individuals: it is a social compact, by which the whole people covenants with each citizen, and each citizen with the whole people, that all shall be governed by certain laws for the common good. It is the duty of the people, therefore, in framing a constitution of government, to provide for an equitable mode of making laws, as well as for an impartial interpretation, and a faithful execution of them; that every man may, at all times, find his security in them.

We, therefore, the people of Massachusetts, acknowledging, with grateful hearts, the goodness of the great Legislator of the universe, in affording us, in the course of His providence, an opportunity, deliberately and peaceably, without fraud, violence or surprise, of entering into an original, explicit, and solemn compact with each other; and of forming a new constitution of civil government, for ourselves and posterity; and devoutly imploring His direction in so interesting a design, do agree upon, ordain and establish the following Declaration of Rights, and Frame of Government, as the Constitution of the Commonwealth of Massachusetts.

PART THE FIRST

A Declaration of the Rights of the Inhabitants of the Commonwealth of Massachusetts:

Article I

All men are born free and equal, and have certain natural, essential, and unalienable rights; among which may be reckoned the right of enjoying and defending their lives and liberties; that of acquiring, possessing, and protecting property; in fine, that of seeking and obtaining their safety and happiness. [Annulled by Amendments, Article CVI]

Article II

It is the right as well as the duty of all men in society, publicly, and at stated seasons to worship the Supreme Being, the great Creator and Preserver of the universe. And no subject shall be hurt, molested, or restrained, in his person, liberty, or estate, for worshipping God in the manner and season most agreeable to the dictates of his own conscience; or for his religious profession or sentiments; provided he doth not disturb the public peace, or obstruct others in their religious worship. [See Amendments, Articles XLVI and XLVIII]

Article III

As the happiness of a people, and the good order and preservation of civil government, essentially depend upon piety, religion and morality; and as these cannot be generally diffused through a community, but by the institution of the public worship of God, and of public instructions in piety, religion and morality: Therefore, to promote their happiness and to secure the good order and preservation of their government, the people of this commonwealth have a right to invest their legislature with power to authorize and require, and the legislature shall, from time to time, authorize and require, the several towns, parishes, precincts, and other bodies politic, or religious societies, to make suitable provision, at their own expense, for the institution of the public worship of God, and for the support and maintenance of public Protestant teachers of piety, religion and morality, in all cases where such provision shall not be made voluntarily.
And the people of this commonwealth have also a right to, and do, invest their legislature with authority to enjoin upon all the subjects an attendance upon the instructions of the public teachers aforesaid, at stated times and seasons, if there be any on whose instructions they can conscientiously and conveniently attend.

Provided, notwithstanding, that the several towns, parishes, precincts, and other bodies politic, or religious societies, shall, at all times, have the exclusive right of electing their public teachers, and of contracting with them for their support and maintenance.

And all moneys paid by the subject to the support of public worship, and of the public teachers aforesaid, shall, if he require it, be uniformly applied to the support of the public teacher or teachers of his own religious sect or denomination, provided there be any on whose instructions he attends; otherwise it may be paid towards the support of the teacher or teachers of the parish or precinct in which the said moneys are raised.
Any every denomination of Christians, demeaning themselves

peaceably, and as good subjects of the commonwealth, shall be equally under the protection of the law: and no subordination of any one sect or denomination to another shall ever be established by law. [Article XI of the Amendments substituted for this]

Article IV

The people of this commonwealth have the sole and exclusive right of governing themselves, as a free, sovereign, and independent state; and do, and forever hereafter shall, exercise and enjoy every power, jurisdiction, and right, which is not, or may not hereafter, be by them expressly delegated to the United States of America in Congress assembled.

Article V

All power residing originally in the people, and being derived from them, the several magistrates and officers of government, vested with authority, whether legislative, executive, or judicial, are their substitutes and agents, and are at all times accountable to them.

Article VI

No man, nor corporation, or association of men, have any other title to obtain advantages, or particular and exclusive privileges, distinct from those of the community, than what arises from the consideration of services rendered to the public; and this title being in nature neither hereditary, nor transmissible to children, or descendants, or relations by blood, the idea of a man born a magistrate, lawgiver, or judge, is absurd and unnatural.

Article VII

Government is instituted for the common good; for the protection, safety, prosperity and happiness of the people; and not for the profit, honor, or private interest of any one man, family, or class of men: Therefore the people alone have an incontestable, unalienable, and indefeasible right to institute government; and to reform, alter, or totally change the same, when their protection, safety, prosperity and happiness require it.

Article VIII

In order to prevent those, who are vested with authority, from becoming oppressors, the people have a right, at such periods and in such manner as they shall establish by their frame of government, to cause their public officers to return to private life; and to fill up vacant places by certain and regular elections and appointments.

Article IX

All elections ought to be free; and all the inhabitants of this commonwealth, having such qualifications as they shall establish by their frame of government, have an equal right to elect officers, and to be elected, for public employments. [See Amendments, Articles XLV and XLVIII, The Initiative, Section 2.] [For compulsory voting, see Amendments, Article LXI] [For use of voting machines at elections, see Amendments, Article XXXVIII] [For absent voting, see Amendments, Article LXXVI]

Article X

Each individual of the society has a right to be protected by it in the enjoyment of his life, liberty and property, according to standing laws. He is obliged, consequently, to contribute his share to the expense of this protection; to give his personal service, or an equivalent, when necessary: but no part of the property of any individual can, with justice, be taken from him, or applied to public uses, without his own consent, or that of the representative body of the people. In fine, the people of this commonwealth are not controllable by any other laws than those to which their constitutional representative body have given their consent. And whenever the public exigencies require that the property of any individual should be appropriated to public uses, he shall receive a reasonable compensation therefor. [See Amendments, Articles XXXIX, XLIII, XLVII, XLVIII, The Initiative, II, Section 2, XLIX, L, LI and XCVII]

Article XI

Every subject of the commonwealth ought to find a certain remedy, by having recourse to the laws, for all injuries or wrongs which he may receive in his person, property, or character. He ought to obtain right and justice freely, and without being obliged to purchase it; completely, and without any denial; promptly, and without delay; conformably to the laws.

Article XII

No subject shall be held to answer for any crimes or offense, until the same is fully and plainly, substantially and formally, described to him; or be compelled to accuse, or furnish evidence against himself. And every subject shall have a right to produce all proofs, that may be favorable to him; to meet the witnesses against him face to face, and to be fully heard in his defense by himself, or his council at his election. And no subject shall be arrested, imprisoned, despoiled, or deprived of his property, immunities, or privileges, put out of the protection of the law, exiled, or deprived of his life, liberty, or estate, but by the judgment of his peers, or the law of the land.

And the legislature shall not make any law, that shall subject any person to a capital or infamous punishment, excepting for the government of the army and navy, without trial by jury. [See Amendments, Article XLVIII, The Initiative, II, Section 2]

Article XIII

In criminal prosecutions, the verification of facts in the vicinity where they happen, is one of the greatest securities of the life, liberty, and property of the citizen.

Article XIV

Every subject has a right to be secure from all unreasonable searches, and seizures, of his person, his houses, his papers, and all his possessions. All warrants, therefore, are contrary to this right, if the cause or foundation of them be not previously supported by oath or affirmation; and if the order in the warrant to a civil officer, to make search in suspected places, or to arrest one or more suspected persons, or to seize their property, be not accompanied with a special designation of the persons or objects of search, arrest, or seizure: and no warrant ought to be issued but in cases, and with the formalities prescribed by the laws. [See Amendments, Article XLVIII, The Initiative, II, Section 2]

Article XV

In all controversies concerning property, and in all suits between two or more persons, except in cases in which it has heretofore been otherways used and practiced, the parties have a right to a trial by jury; and this method of procedure shall be held sacred, unless, in causes arising on the high seas, and such as relate to mariners' wages, the legislature shall hereafter find it necessary to alter it. [See Amendments, Article XLVIII, The Initiative, II, Section 2]

Article XVI

The liberty of the press is essential to the security of freedom in a state: it ought not, therefore, to be restrained in this commonwealth. [See Amendments, Article XLVIII, The Initiative, II, Section 2] [Annulled and superseded by Amendments, Article LXXVII]

Article XVII

The people have a right to keep and to bear arms for the common defence. And as, in time of peace, armies are dangerous to liberty, they ought not to be maintained without the consent of the legislature; and the military power shall always be held in an exact subordination to the civil authority, and be governed by it.

Article XVIII

A frequent recurrence to the fundamental principles of the constitution, and a constant adherence to those of piety, justice, moderation, temperance, industry, and frugality, are absolutely necessary to preserve the advantages of liberty, and to maintain a free government. The people ought, consequently, to have a particular attention to all those principles, in the choice of their officers and representatives: and they have a right to require of their lawgivers and magistrates, an exact and constant observance of them, in the formation and execution of the laws necessary for the good administration of the commonwealth.

Article XIX

The people have a right, in an orderly and peaceable manner, to assemble to consult upon the common good; give instructions to their representatives, and to request of the legislative body, by the way of addresses, petitions, or remonstrances, redress of the wrongs done them, and of the grievances they suffer. [See Amendments, Article XLVIII, The Initiative, II, Section 2]

Article XX

The power of suspending the laws, or the execution of the laws, ought never to be exercised but by the legislature, or by authority derived from it, to be exercised in such particular cases only as the legislature shall expressly provide for. [See Amendments, Article XLVIII, I, Definition and LXXXIX]

Article XXI

The freedom of deliberation, speech and debate, in either house of the legislature, is so essential to the rights of the people, that it cannot be the foundation of any accusation or prosecution, action or complaint, in any other court or place whatsoever. [See Amendments, Article XLVIII, The Initiative, II, Section 2]

Article XXII

The legislature ought frequently to assemble for the redress of grievances, for correcting, strengthening and confirming the laws, and for making new laws, as the common good may require.

Article XXIII

No subsidy, charge, tax, impost, or duties, ought to be established, fixed, laid, or levied, under any pretext whatsoever, without the consent of the people or their representatives in the legislature.

Article XXIV

Laws made to punish for actions done before the existence of such laws, and which have not been declared crimes by preceding laws, are unjust, oppressive, and inconsistent with the fundamental principles of a free government.

Article XXV

No subject ought, in any case, or in any time, to be declared guilty of treason or felony by the legislature.

Article XXVI.

No magistrate or court of law, shall demand excessive bail or sureties, impose excessive fines, or inflict cruel or unusual punishments. [See Amendments, Article XLVIII, The Initiative, II, Section 2, and CXVI]

Article XXVII

In time of peace, no soldier ought to be quartered in any house without the consent of the owner; and in time of war, such quarters ought not to be made but by the civil magistrate, in a manner ordained by the legislature.

Article XXVIII

No person can in any case be subject to law-martial, or to any penalties or pains, by virtue of that law, except those employed in the army or navy, and except the militia in actual service, but by authority of the legislature. [See Amendments, Article XLVIII, The Initiative, II, Section 2]

Article XXIX.

It is essential to the preservation of the rights of every individual, his life, liberty, property, and character, that there be an impartial interpretation of the laws, and administration of justice. It is the right of every citizen to be tried by judges as free, impartial and independent as the lot of humanity will admit. It is, therefore, not only the best policy, but for the security of the rights of the people, and of every citizen, that the judges of the supreme judicial court should hold their offices as long as they behave themselves well; and that they should have honorable salaries ascertained and established by standing laws. [See Amendments, Article. XLVIII, The Initiative, II, Section 2, and The Referendum, III, Section 2, LXVIII and XCVIII]

Article XXX

In the government of this commonwealth, the legislative department shall never exercise the executive and judicial powers, or either of them: the executive shall never exercise the legislative and judicial powers, or either of them: the judicial shall never exercise the legislative and executive powers, or either of them: to the end it may be a government of laws and not of men.

PART THE SECOND

The Frame of Government:

The people, inhabiting the territory formerly called the Province of Massachusetts Bay, do hereby solemnly and mutually agree with each other, to form themselves into a free, sovereign, and independent body politic, or state by the name of "THE COMMONWEALTH OF MASSACHUSETTS"

Chapter I: LEGISLATIVE POWER

Section I: The General Court

Article I

The department of legislation shall be formed by two branches, a Senate and House of Representatives: each of which shall have a negative on the other.

The legislative body shall assemble every year [on the last Wednesday in May, and at such other times as they shall judge necessary; and shall dissolve and be dissolved on the day next preceding the said last Wednesday in May;] and shall be stiled, The General Court of Massachusetts. [See Amendments, Articles X, LXXII, and LXXV]

Article II

No bill or resolve of the senate or house of representatives shall become a law, and have force as such, until it shall have been laid before the governor for his revisal; and if he, upon such revision, approve thereof, he shall signify his approbation by signing the same. But if he have any objection to the passing of such bill or resolve, he shall return the same, together with his objections thereto, in writing, to the senate or house of representatives, in whichsoever the same shall have originated; who shall enter the objections sent down by the governor, at large, on their records, and proceed to reconsider the said bill or resolve. But if after such reconsideration, two thirds of the said senate or house of representatives, shall, notwithstanding the said objections, agree to pass the same, it shall, together with the objections, be sent to the other branch of the legislature, where it shall also be reconsidered, and if approved by two thirds of the members present, shall have the force of a law: but in all such cases, the votes of both houses shall be determined by yeas and nays; and the names of the persons voting for, or against, the said bill or resolve, shall be entered upon the public records of the commonwealth.

[And in order to prevent unnecessary delays, if any bill or resolve shall not be returned by the governor within five days after it shall have been presented, the same shall have the force of a law.] [See Amendments, Articles I, XLVIII, LIV, LXIII, Section 5, and XC, Section 1]

Article III

The general court shall forever have full power and authority to erect and constitute judicatories and courts of record, or other courts, to be held in the name of the commonwealth, for the hearing, trying, and determining of all manner of crimes, offenses, pleas, processes, plaints, actions, matters, causes and things, whatsoever, arising or happening within the commonwealth, or between or concerning persons inhabiting, or residing, or brought within the same, whether the same be criminal or civil, or whether the said crimes be capital or not capital, and whether the said pleas be real, personal, or mixed; and for the awarding and making out of execution thereupon. To which courts and judicatories are hereby given and granted full power and authority, from time to time, to administer oaths or affirmations, for the better discovery of truth in any matter in controversy or depending before them. [See Amendments, Article XLVIII, The Initiative, II, Section 2, and The Referendum, III, Section 2]

Article IV

And further, full power and authority are hereby given and granted to the said general court, from time to time, to make, ordain, and establish, all manner of wholesome and reasonable orders, laws, statutes, and ordinances, directions and instructions, either with penalties or without; so as the same be not repugnant or contrary to this constitution, as they shall judge to be for the good and welfare of this commonwealth, and for the government and ordering thereof, and of the subjects of the same, and for the necessary support and defence of the government thereof; and to name and settle annually, or provide by fixed laws, for the naming and settling all civil officers within the said commonwealth; the election and constitution of whom are not hereafter in this form of government otherwise provided for; and to set forth the several duties, powers, and limits, of the several civil and military officers of this commonwealth, and the forms of such oaths or affirmations as shall be respectively administered unto them for the execution of their several offices and places, so as the same be not repugnant or contrary to this constitution; and to impose and levy proportional and reasonable assessments, rates, and taxes, upon all the inhabitants of, and persons resident, and estates lying, within the said commonwealth; and also to impose and levy, reasonable duties and excises, upon any produce, goods, wares, merchandise, and commodities, whatsoever, brought into, produced, manufactured, or being within the same; to be issued and disposed of by warrant, under the hand of the governor of this commonwealth for the time being, with the advice and consent of the council, for the public service, in the necessary defence and support of the government of the said commonwealth, and the protection and preservation of the subjects thereof, according to such acts as are or shall be in force within the same.

And while the public charges of government, or any part thereof, shall be assessed on polls and estates, in the manner that has hitherto been practiced, in order that such assessments may be made with equality, there shall be a valuation of estates within the commonwealth taken anew once in every ten years at least, and as much oftener as the general court shall order. [See Amendments, Articles XLI, XLIV, XCIX and CXII]

For the authority of the general court to charter cities and establish limited town meeting form of government, see Amendments, Articles II and LXX.

For power of the general court to establish voting precincts in towns, see Amendments. Article XXIX.

For additional taxing power given to the general court, see Amendments, Articles XLI and XLIV.

For the authority of the general court to take land, etc., for relieving congestion of population and providing homes for citizens, see Amendments, Article XLIII.

For the power given the general court to provide by law for absentee and compulsory voting, see Amendments, Article XLV, Amendments, Article LXI and Amendments, Article LXXVI.

For the power of the general court to determine the manner of providing and distributing the necessaries of life, etc., during time of war, public distress, etc., by the Commonwealth and the cities and towns, therein, see Amendments, Article LXVII.

For provisions relative to taking the vote on emergency measures, see Amendments, Article XLVIII, The Referendum, II, and LXVII.

For new provisions authorizing the general court to provide for the taking of lands for certain public uses, see Amendments, Article XLIX.

For provisions authorizing the general court to take a recess or recesses amounting to not more than thirty days, see Amendments, Article LII.

For new provision authorizing the governor to return a bill with a recommendation of amendment, see Amendments, Article LVI.

For the power of the general court to limit the use of construction of buildings, see Amendments, Article LX.

For new provisions relative to the biennial election of senators and representatives and their terms of office, see Amendments, Article LXIV.

For new provisions that no person elected to the general court shall be appointed to any office which was created or the emoluments of which were increased during the term for which he was elected, nor received additional salary or compensation for service upon recess committees or commissions, see Amendments, Article LXV.

For the power of the general court to prescribe the terms and conditions upon which a pardon may be granted in the case of a felony, see Amendments, Article LXXIII.

Chapter I. Section II: The Senate

Article I.

There shall be annually elected, by the freeholders and other inhabitants of this commonwealth, qualified as in this constitution is provided, forty persons to be councillors and senators for the year ensuing their election; to be chosen by the inhabitants of the districts, into which the commonwealth may from time to time be divided by the general court for that purpose: and the general court in assigning the numbers to be elected by the respective districts, shall govern themselves by the proportion of the public taxes paid by the said districts; and timely make known to the inhabitants of the commonwealth, the limits of each district, and the number of councillors and senators to be chosen therein; provided that the number of such districts shall never be less than thirteen; and that no district be so large as to entitle the same to choose more than six senators. [See Amendments, Articles XIII, XVI, XXII, LXIV, LXXI, CXII, CI and CIX.]

And the several counties in this commonwealth shall, until the general court shall determine it necessary to alter the said districts, be districts for the choice of councillors and senators, (except that the counties of Dukes County and Nantucket shall form one district for that purpose) and shall elect the following number for councillors and senators, viz.: -- Suffolk, Six; Essex, six; Middlesex, five; Hampshire, four; Plymouth, three; Barnstable, one; Bristol, three; York, two; Dukes County and Nantucket, one; Worcester, five; Cumberland, one; Lincoln, one; Berkshire, two.]

Article II.

The senate shall be the first branch of the legislature; and the senators shall be chosen in the following manner, viz. there shall be a meeting on the [first Monday in April], [annually], forever, of the inhabitants of each town in the several counties of this commonwealth; to be called by the selectmen, and warned in due course of law, at least seven days before the [first Monday in April], for the purpose of electing persons to be senators and councillors; [and at such meetings every male inhabitant of twenty-one years of age and upwards, having a freehold estate within the commonwealth, of the annual income of three pounds, or any estate of the value of sixty pounds, shall have a right to give in his vote for the senators for the district of which he is an inhabitant.] And to remove all doubts concerning the meaning of the word "inhabitant" in this constitution, every person shall be considered as an inhabitant, for the purpose of electing and being elected into any office, or place within this state, in that town, district or plantation where he dwelleth, or hath his home. [See Amendments, Articles II, III, X, XV, XX, XXII, XXIII, XXVI, XXVIII, XXX, XXXI, XXXII, XLV, LXIV, LXXI, LXXVI, LXXX, XCII, XCIII, XCIV, XCV, C,, CI and CIX]

The selectmen of the several towns shall preside at such meetings impartially; and shall receive the votes of all the inhabitants of such towns present and qualified to vote for senators, and shall sort and count them in open town meeting, and in presence of the town clerk, who shall make a fair record, in presence of the selectmen, and in open town meeting, of the name of every person voted for, and of the number of votes against his name: and a fair copy of this record shall be attested by the selectmen and the town clerk, and shall be sealed up, directed to the secretary of the commonwealth for the time being, with a superscription, expressing the purport of the contents thereof, and delivered by the town clerk of such towns, to the sheriff of the county in which such town lies, thirty days at least before [the last Wednesday in May] [annually]; or it shall be delivered into the secretary's office seventeen days at least before the said [last Wednesday in May]: and the sheriff of each county shall deliver all such certificates by him received, into the secretary's office, seventeen days before the said [last Wednesday in May]. [See Amendments, Articles II, and X]

And the inhabitants of plantations unincorporated, qualified as this constitution provides, who are or shall be empowered and required to assess taxes upon themselves toward the support of government, shall have the same privilege of voting for councillors and senators in the plantations where they reside, as town inhabitants have in their respective towns; [and the plantation meetings for that purpose shall be held annually on the same first Monday in April], at such place in the plantations respectively, as the assessors thereof shall direct; which assessors shall have like authority for notifying the electors, collecting and returning the votes, as the selectmen and town clerks have in their several towns, by this constitution. And all other persons living in places unincorporated (qualified as aforesaid) who shall be assessed to the support of government by the assessors of an adjacent town, shall have the privilege of giving in their votes for councillors and senators in the town where they shall be assessed, and be notified of the place of meeting by the selectmen of the town where they shall be assessed, for that purpose accordingly. [See Amendments, Articles XV and LXIV]

Article III

And that there may be a due convention of senators on the [last Wednesday in May] [annually,] the governor with five of the council, for the time being, shall, as soon as may be, examine the returned copies of such records; and fourteen days before the said day he shall issue his summons to such persons as shall appear to be chosen by [a majority of] voters, to attend on that day, and take their seats accordingly: provided nevertheless, that for the first year the said returned copies shall be examined by the president and five of the council of the former constitution of government; and the said president shall, in like manner, issue his summons to the persons so elected, that they may take their seats as aforesaid. [See Amendments, Articles X, XIV, LXIV, LXXII and LXXV.]

Article IV.

The senate shall be the final judge of the elections, returns and qualifications of their own members, as pointed out in the constitution; and shall, [on the said last Wednesday in May] [annually] determine and declare who are elected by each district, to be senators [by a majority of votes; and in case there shall not appear to be the full number of senators returned elected by a majority of votes for any district, the deficiency shall be supplied in the following manner, viz.: The members of the house of representatives, and such senators as shall be declared elected, shall take the names of such persons as shall be found to have the highest number of votes in such district, and not elected, amounting to twice the number of senators wanting, if there be so many voted for; and out of these shall elect by ballot a number of senators sufficient to fill up the vacancies in such district; and in this manner all such vacancies shall be filled up in every district of the commonwealth; and in like manner all vacancies in the senate, arising by death, removal out of the state, or otherwise, shall be supplied as soon as may be, after such vacancies shall happen.] [See Amendments, Articles X, XIV and XXIV]

Article V.

Provided nevertheless, that no person shall be capable of being elected as a senator, [who is not seised in his own right of a freehold within this commonwealth, of the value of three hundred pounds at least, or possessed of personal estate to the value of six hundred pounds at least, or of both to the amount of the same sum, and] who has not been an inhabitant of this commonwealth for the space of five years immediately preceding his election, and at the time of his election, he shall be an inhabitant in the district for which he shall be chosen. [See Amendments, Articles XIII, XXII, LXXI, XCII, CI and CIX]

Article VI

The senate shall have power to adjourn themselves, provided such adjournments do not exceed two days at a time. [See Amendments, Articles LII and CII]

Article VII

The senate shall choose its own president, appoint its own officers, and determine its own rules of proceedings.

Article VIII

The senate shall be a court with full authority to hear and determine all impeachments made by the house of representatives, against any officer or officers of the commonwealth, for misconduct and mal-administration in their offices. But previous to the trial of every impeachment the members of the senate shall respectively be sworn, truly and impartially to try and determine the charge in question, according to evidence. Their judgment, however shall not extend further than to removal from office and disqualification to hold or enjoy any place of honor, trust, or profit, under this commonwealth: but the party so convicted, shall be, nevertheless, liable to indictment, trial, judgment, and punishment, according to the laws of the land.

Article IX.

[Not less than sixteen members of the senate shall constitute a quorum for doing business.] [See Amendments, Articles XXII and XXXIII]

Chapter I. Section III: House of Representatives

Article I.

There shall be, in the legislature of this commonwealth, a representation of the people, [annually] elected, and founded upon the principle of equality. [See Amendments, Article LXIV]

Article II.

[And in order to provide for a representation of the citizens of this commonwealth, founded upon the principle of equality, every corporate town containing one hundred and fifty ratable polls, may elect one representative: every corporate town, containing three hundred and seventy-five ratable polls may elect two representatives: every corporate town containing six hundred ratable polls, may elect three representatives: and proceeding in that manner, making two hundred and twenty-five ratable polls, the mean increasing number for every additional representative. [See Amendments, Articles XII, XIII, XXI, LXXI, XCII, CI and CIX]

Provided nevertheless, that each town now incorporated, not having one hundred and fifty ratable polls, may elect one representative: but no place shall hereafter be incorporated with the privilege of electing a representative, unless there are within the same one hundred and fifty ratable polls]

And the house of representatives shall have power from time to time to impose fines upon such towns as shall neglect to choose and return members to the same, agreeably to this constitution.

[The expenses of traveling to the general assembly, and returning home, once in every session, and no more, shall be paid by the government, out of the public treasury, to every member who shall attend as seasonably as he can, in the judgment of the house, and does not depart without leave.] [See Amendments, Article XXXV]

Article III.

Every member of the house of representatives shall be chosen by written votes; [and for one year at least next preceding his election, shall have been an inhabitant of, and have been seized in his own right of a freehold of the value of one hundred pounds within the town he shall be chosen to represent, or any ratable estate to the value of two hundred pounds; and he shall cease to represent the said town immediately on his ceasing to be qualified as aforesaid.] [See Amendments, Articles XIII, XXI, LXXI, XCII, CI and CIX]

Article IV.

[Every male person, being twenty-one years of age, and resident in any particular town in this commonwealth for the space of one year next preceding, having a freehold estate within the same town, of the annual income of three pounds, or any estate of the value of sixty pounds, shall have a right to vote in the choice of a representative, or representatives for the said town.] [See Amendments, Articles III, XX, XXIII, XXVI, XXVIII, XXX, XXXI, XXXII, XLV, LXXVI, XCIII, XCIV, XCV, and C]

Article V.

[The members of the house of representatives shall be chosen annually in the month of May, ten days at least before the last Wednesday of that month.] [See Amendments, Articles X, XV and LXIV]

Article VI.

The house of representatives shall be the grand inquest of this commonwealth; and all impeachments made by them, shall be heard and tried by the senate.

Article VII.

All money bills shall originate in the house of representatives; but the senate may propose or concur with amendments, as on other bills.

Article VIII.

The house of representatives shall have power to adjourn themselves; provided such adjournment shall not exceed two days at a time. [See Amendments, Articles LII and CII]

Article IX.

[Not less than sixty members of the house of representatives, shall constitute a quorum for doing business.] [See Amendments, ArticlesXXI and XXXIII]

Article X.

The house of representatives shall be the judge of the returns, elections, and qualifications of its own members, as pointed out in the constitution; shall choose their own speaker; appoint their own officers, and settle the rules and orders of proceeding in their own house: They shall have authority to punish by imprisonment, every person, not a member, who shall be guilty of disrespect to the house, by any disorderly, or contemptuous behavior, in its presence; or who, in the town where the general court is sitting, and during the time of its sitting, shall threaten harm to the body or estate of any of its members, for any thing said or done in the house; or who shall assault any of them therefor; or who shall assault, or arrest, any witness, or other person, ordered to attend the house, in his way in going or returning; or who shall rescue any person arrested by the order of the house.

And no member of the house of representatives shall be arrested, or held to bail on mesne process, during his going unto, returning from, or his attending the general assembly.

Article XI.

The senate shall have the same powers in the like cases; and the governor and council shall have the same authority to punish in like cases. Provided that no imprisonment on the warrant or order of the governor, council, senate, or house of representatives, for either of the above described offences, be for a term exceeding thirty days.

And the senate and house of representatives may try, and determine, all cases where their rights and privileges are concerned, and which, by the constitution, they have authority to try and determine, by committees of their own members, or in such other way as they may respectively think best.

Chapter II. EXECUTIVE POWER

Section I: The Governor

Article I.

There shall be a supreme executive magistrate, who shall be styled, The Governor of the Commonwealth of Massachusetts; and whose title shall be -- His Excellency.

Article II.

The governor shall be chosen [annually]; and no person shall be eligible to this office, unless at the time of his election, he shall have been an inhabitant of this commonwealth for seven years next preceding; [and unless he shall at the same time, be seised in his own right, of a freehold within the commonwealth of the value of one thousand pounds; and unless he shall declare himself to be of the Christian religion.] [See Amendments, Articles VII,XXXIV, LXIV and LXXX]

Article III.

Those persons who shall be qualified to vote for senators and representatives within the several towns of this commonwealth, shall, at a meeting to be called for that purpose, on the [first Monday of April annually], give in their votes for a governor, to the selectmen, who shall preside at such meetings; and the town clerk, in the presence and with the assistance of the selectmen, shall, in open town meeting, sort and count the votes, and form a list of the persons voted for, with the number of votes for each person against his name; and shall make a fair record of the same in the town books, and a public declaration thereof in the said meeting; and shall, in the presence of the inhabitants, seal up copies of the said list, attested by him and the selectmen, and transmit the same to the sheriff of the county thirty days at least before the [last Wednesday in May]; and the sheriff shall transmit the same to the secretary's office, seventeen days at least before the said [last Wednesday in May]; or the selectmen may cause returns of the same to be made to the office of the secretary of the commonwealth, seventeen days at least before the said day; and the secretary shall lay the same before the senate and the house of representatives, on the [last Wednesday in May], to be by them examined: and in case of an election by a [majority] of all the votes returned, the choice shall be by them declared and published. But if no person shall have a [majority] of votes, the house of representatives shall, by ballot, elect two out of four persons who had the highest number of votes, if so many shall have been voted for, but, if otherwise, out of the number voted for; and make return to the senate of the two persons so elected; on which the senate shall proceed, by ballot, to elect one, who shall be declared governor. [See Amendments, Articles II, X, XIV, XV, XLV, LXIV, LXXVI and LXXX]

Article IV.

The governor shall have authority from time to time, at his discretion, to assemble and call together the councillors of this commonwealth for the time being; and the governor with the said councillors, or five of them at least, shall, and may, from time to time, hold and keep a council, for the ordering and directing the affairs of the commonwealth, agreeably to the constitution and the laws of the land.

Article V.

The governor, with advice of council, shall have full power and authority, during the session of the general court to adjourn or prorogue the same to any time the two houses shall desire; [and to dissolve the same on the day next preceding the last Wednesday in May;] and, in the recess of the said court, to prorogue the same from time to time, not exceeding ninety days in any one recess; and to call it together sooner than the time to which it may be adjourned or prorogued, if the welfare of the commonwealth shall require the same: and in case of any infectious distemper prevailing in the place where the said court is next at any time to convene, or any other cause happening whereby danger may arise to the health or lives of the members from their attendance, he may direct the session to be held at some other, the most convenient place within the state.
[And the governor shall dissolve the said general court on the day next preceding the last Wednesday in May.] [See Amendments, Articles X, LXXII and LXXV]

Article VI.

In cases of disagreement between the two houses, with regard to the necessity, expediency or time of adjournment, or prorogation, the governor, with the advice of the council, shall have a right to adjourn or prorogue the general court, not exceeding ninety days, as he shall determine the public good shall require.

Article VII.

[The governor of this commonwealth for the time being, shall be the commander in chief of the army and navy, and of all the military forces of the state, by sea and land, and shall have full power by himself, or by any commander, or other officer or officers, from time to time, to train, instruct, exercise and govern the militia and navy; and, for the special defence and safety of the commonwealth, to assemble in martial array, and put in warlike posture, the inhabitants thereof, and to lead and conduct them, and with them to encounter, repel, resist, expel and pursue, by force of arms, as well by sea as by land, within or without the limits of this commonwealth, and also to kill, slay and destroy, if necessary, and conquer, by all fitting ways, enterprises, and means whatsoever, all and every such person and persons as shall, at any time hereafter, in a hostile manner, attempt or enterprise the destruction, invasion, detriment, or annoyance of this commonwealth; and to use and exercise, over the army and navy, and over the militia in actual service, the law martial, in time of war or invasion, and also in time of rebellion, declared by the legislature to exist, as occasion shall necessarily require; and to take and surprise by all ways and means whatsoever, all and every such person or persons, with their ships, arms, ammunition and other goods, as shall, in a hostile manner, invade, or attempt the invading, conquering, or annoying this commonwealth; and that the governor be intrusted with all these and other powers, incident to the offices of captain-general and commander in chief, and admiral, to be exercised agreeably to the rules and regulations of the constitution, and the laws of the land, and not otherwise. Provided, that the said governor shall not, at any time hereafter, by virtue of any power by this constitution granted, or hereafter to be granted to him by the legislature, transport any of the inhabitants of this commonwealth, or oblige them to march out of the limits of the same, without their free and voluntary consent, or the consent of the general court; except so far as may be necessary to march or transport them by land or water, for the defence of such part of the state, to which they cannot otherwise conveniently have access.] [Annulled and superseded by See Amendments, Article LIV]

Article VIII.

[The power of pardoning offences, except such as persons may be convicted of before the senate by an impeachment of the house, shall be in the governor, by and with the advice of council: but no charter of pardon, granted by the governor, with advice of the council before conviction, shall avail the party pleading the same, notwithstanding any general or particular expressions contained therein, descriptive of the offence or offences intended to be pardoned.] [Annulled and superseded by Amendments, Article LXXIII]

Article IX.

All judicial officers, [the attorney-general,] the solicitor-general, [all sheriffs,] coroners, [and registers of probate,] shall be nominated and appointed by the governor, by and with the advice and consent of the council; and every such nomination shall be made by the governor, and made at least seven days prior to such appointment. [See Amendments, Articles XVII, [See Amendments, Article XLVIII, The Initiative, II, Section 2], The Referendum, III, Section 2, and LXIV] [For provision as to election of sheriffs, registers of probate, etc., see Amendments, Article XIX] [For provision as to the appointment of notaries public, see Amendments, Articles IV, LVII and LXIX, Section 2]

Article X.

[The captains and subalterns of the militia, shall be elected by the written votes of the train band and alarm list of their respective companies, of twenty-one years of age and upwards: the field officers of regiments shall be elected by the written votes of the captains and subalterns of their respective regiments: the brigadiers shall be elected in like manner, by the field officers of their respective brigades: and such officers, so elected, shall be commissioned by the governor, who shall determine their rank. [See Amendments, Article V]

The legislature shall, by standing laws, direct the time and manner of convening the electors, and of collecting votes, and of certifying to the governor, the officers elected.

The major-generals shall be appointed by the senate and house of representatives, each having a negative upon the other; and be commissioned by the governor. [See Amendments, Article IV]

And if the electors of brigadiers, field officers, captains or subalterns, shall neglect or refuse to make such elections, after being duly notified, according to the laws for the time being, then the governor, with advice of council, shall appoint suitable persons to fill such offices.

And no officer, duly commissioned to command in the militia, shall be removed from his office, but by the address of both houses to the governor, or by fair trial in court-martial pursuant to the laws of the commonwealth for the time being. [See Amendments, Article IV]

The commanding officers of regiments shall appoint their adjutants and quartermasters; the brigadiers their brigade-majors; and the major-generals their aids; and the governor shall appoint the adjutant-general.

The governor, with advice of council, shall appoint all officers of the continental army, whom by the confederation of the United States it is provided that this commonwealth shall appoint, as also all officers of forts and garrisons.

The divisions of the militia into brigades, regiments and companies, made in pursuance of the militia laws now in force, shall be considered as the proper divisions of the militia of this commonwealth, until the same shall be altered in pursuance of some future law.] [Annulled and superseded by Amendments, Article LIII]

Article XI.

No moneys shall be issued out of the treasury of this commonwealth, and disposed of (except such sums as may be appropriated for the redemption of bills of credit or treasurer's notes, or for the payment of interest arising thereon) but by warrant under the hand of the governor for the time being, with the advice and consent of the council, for the necessary defence and support of the commonwealth; and for the protection and preservation of the inhabitants thereof, agreeably to the acts and resolves of the general court. [See Amendments, Article XLVIII, The Initiative, II, Section 2, and The Referendum, III, Section 2]

Article XII.

All public boards, [the commissary-general,] all superintending officers of public magazines and stores, belonging to this commonwealth, and all commanding officers of forts and garrisons within the same, shall once in every three months, officially, and without requisition, and at other times, when required by the governor, deliver to him an account of all goods, stores, provisions, ammunition, cannon with their appendages, and small arms with their accoutrements, and of all other public property whatever under their care respectively; distinguishing the quantity, number, quality and kind of each, as particularly as may be; together with the condition of such forts and garrisons and the said commanding officer shall exhibit to the governor, when required by him, true and exact plans of such forts, and of the land and sea or harbor or harbors adjacent.

And the said boards, and all public officers, shall communicate to the governor, as soon as may be after receiving the same, all letters, despatches, and intelligences of a public nature, which shall be directed to them respectively. [See Amendments, Article LIII]

Article XIII.

As the public good requires that the governor should not be under the undue influence of any of the members of the general court by a dependence on them for his support, that he should in all cases, act with freedom for the benefit of the public, that he should not have his attention necessarily diverted from that object to his private concerns -- and that he should maintain the dignity of the commonwealth in the character of its chief magistrate, it is necessary that he should have an honorable stated salary, of a fixed and permanent value, amply sufficient for those purposes, and established by standing laws: and it shall be among the first acts of the general court, after the commencement of this constitution, to establish such salary by law accordingly.

Permanent and honorable salaries shall also be established by law for the justices of the supreme judicial court.
And if it shall be found that any of the salaries aforesaid, so established, are insufficient, they shall, from time to time be enlarged as the general court shall judge proper. [See Amendments, Article XLVIII, The Initiative, II, Section 2, and The Referendum, III, Section 2]

Chapter II. Section II: Lieutenant-Governor

Article I.

There shall be [annually] elected a lieutenant governor of the commonwealth of Massachusetts, whose title shall be, His Honor and who shall be qualified, in point of [religion, property,] and residence in the commonwealth, in the same manner with the governor: and the day and manner of his election, and the qualifications of the electors, shall be the same as are required in the election of a governor. The return of the votes for this officer, and the declaration of his election, shall be in the same manner: and if no one person shall be found to have [a majority] of all the votes returned, the vacancy shall be filled by the senate and house of representatives, in the same manner as the governor is to be elected, in case no one person shall have [a majority] of the votes of the people to be governor. [See Amendments, Articles VII, XIV, XXXIV, LXIV and LXXX]

Article II.

The governor, and in his absence the lieutenant governor, shall be president of the council, but shall have no vote in council: and the lieutenant governor shall always be a member of the council except when the chair of the governor shall be vacant.

Article III.

Whenever the chair of the governor shall be vacant, by reason of his death, or absence from the commonwealth, or otherwise, the lieutenant governor, for the time being, shall, during such vacancy, perform all the duties incumbent upon the governor, and shall have and exercise all the powers and authorities, which by this constitution the governor is vested with, when personally present. [See Amendments, Articles LV]

Chapter II. Section III: Council, and the Manner of settling Elections by the Legislature

Article I.

There shall be a council for advising the governor in the executive part of government, to consist of [nine] persons besides the lieutenant governor, whom the governor, for the time being, shall have full power and authority, from time to time, at his discretion, to assemble and call together. And the governor, with the said councillors, or five of them at least, shall and may, from time to time, hold and keep a council, for the ordering and directing the affairs of the commonwealth, according to the laws of the land. [See Amendments, Article XVI]

Article II.

[Nine councillors shall be annually chosen from among the persons returned for councillors and senators, on the last Wednesday in May, by the joint ballot of the senators and representatives assembled in one room: and in case there shall not be found upon the first choice, the whole number of nine persons who will accept a seat in the council, the deficiency shall be made up by the electors aforesaid from among the people at large; and the number of senators left shall constitute the senate for the year. The seats of the persons thus elected from the senate, and accepting the trust, shall be vacated in the senate.] [See Amendments, Articles X, XIII, XXV, LXIV.] [Superseded by Amendments, Article XVI]

Article III.

The councillors, in the civil arrangements of the commonwealth, shall have rank next after the lieutenant governor.
Article IV.
[Not more than two councillors shall be chosen out of any one district of this commonwealth] [Superseded by Amendments, Article XVI]

Article IV.

[Not more than two councillors shall be chosen out of any one district of this commonwealth.] [Superseded by Amendments, Art XVI]

Article V.

The resolutions and advice of the council shall be recorded in a register, and signed by the members present; and this record may be called for at any time by either house of the legislature; and any member of the council may insert his opinion, contrary to the resolution of the majority.

Article VI.

[Whenever the office of the governor and lieutenant governor shall be vacant, by reason of death, absence, or otherwise, then the council, or the major part of them, shall during such vacancy have full power and authority to do, and execute, all and every such acts, matters and things, as the governor or the lieutenant governor might or could, by virtue of this constitution, do or execute, if they or either of them, were personally present.]
[Annulled and superseded by Amendments, Article LV]

Article VII.

[And whereas the elections appointed to be made by this constitution, on the last Wednesday in May annually, by the two houses of the legislature, may not be completed on that day, the said elections may be adjourned from day to day until the same shall be completed. And the order of elections shall be as follows: the vacancies in the senate, if any, shall first be filled up; the governor and lieutenant governor shall then be elected, provided there should be no choice of them by the people: and afterwards the two houses shall proceed to the election of the council.] [See Amendments, Article XIV.] [Superseded by Amendments, Articles XVI and XXV]

Chapter II. Section IV: Secretary, Treasurer, Commissary, etc.

Article I.

[The secretary, treasurer and receiver-general, and the commissary-general, notaries public, and naval officers, shall be chosen annually, by joint ballot of the senators and representatives in one room. And that the citizens of this commonwealth may be assured, from time to time, that the moneys remaining in the public treasury, upon the settlement and liquidation of the public accounts, are their property, no man shall be eligible as treasurer and receiver-general more than five years successively.] [See Amendments, Articles XVII, LXIV, LXXIX, LXXX and LXXXII] [For provision as to appointment of notaries public and the commisary-general, see Amendments, Articles IV, LIII and LVII; see also Amendments, Article LXIX]

Article II.

The records of the commonwealth shall be kept in the office of the secretary, who may appoint his deputies, for whose conduct he shall be accountable, and he shall attend the governor and council, the senate and house of representatives, in person, or by his deputies, as they shall respectively require.

Chapter III. Judiciary Power

Article I.

The tenure, that all commission officers shall by law have in their offices, shall be expressed in their respective commissions. All judicial officers, duly appointed, commissioned and sworn, shall hold their offices during good behavior, excepting such concerning whom there is different provision made in this constitution: provided nevertheless, the governor, with consent of the council, may remove them upon the address of both houses of the legislature. [For tenure, etc., of judges, see Amendments, Article XLVIII, The Initiative, II, Section 2 and The Referendum, III, Section 2] [For retirement of judicial officers, see Amendments, Article LVIII] [For removal of justices of the peace and notaries public, see Amendments, Article XXXVII] [Annulled by Amendments, Article XCVIII]

Article II.

[Each branch of the legislature, as well as the governor and council, shall have authority to require the opinions of the justices of the supreme judicial court, upon important questions of law, and upon solemn occasions.] [Amended and superseded by Amendments, Article LXXXV]

Article III.

In order that the people may not suffer from the long continuance in place of any justice of the peace, who shall fail of discharging the important duties of his office with ability or fidelity, all commissions of justices of the peace shall expire and become void, in the term of seven years from their respective dates; and upon the expiration of any commission, the same may, if necessary, be renewed, or another person appointed, as shall most conduce to the well-being of the commonwealth. [See Amendments, Article XXXVII]

Article IV.

The judges of probate of wills, and for granting letters of administration, shall hold their courts at such place or places, on fixed days, as the convenience of the people shall require; and the legislature shall, from time to time, hereafter appoint such times and places; until which appointments, the said courts shall be holden at the times and places which the respective judges shall direct.

Article V.

All causes of marriage, divorce, and alimony, and all appeals from the judges of probate shall be heard and determined by the governor and council, until the legislature shall, by law, make other provision.

Chapter IV. Delegates To Congress

[The delegates of this commonwealth to the congress of the United States, shall, some time in the month of June annually, be elected by the joint ballot of the senate and house of representatives, assembled together in one room; to serve in congress for one year, to commence on the first Monday in November then next ensuing. They shall have commissions under the hand of the governor, and the great seal of the commonwealth; but may be recalled at any time within the year, and others chosen and commissioned, in the same manner, in their stead.] [Annulled by the adoption of the Constitution of the United States, July 26, 1788.]

Chapter V. The University at Cambridge, and Encouragement of Literature, etc.

Section I. The University:

Article I.

Whereas our wise and pious ancestors, so early as the year one thousand six hundred and thirty-six, laid the foundation of Harvard College, in which university many persons of great eminence have, by the blessing of God, been initiated in those arts and sciences, which qualified them for public employments, both in church and state: and whereas the encouragement of arts and sciences, and all good literature, tends to the honor of God, the advantage of the Christian religion, and the great benefit of this and the other United States of America -- it is declared, that the President and Fellows of Harvard College, in their corporate capacity, and their successors in that capacity, their officers and servants, shall have, hold, use, exercise and enjoy, all the powers, authorities, rights, liberties, privileges, immunities and franchises, which they now have or are entitled to have, hold, use, exercise and enjoy: and the same are hereby ratified and confirmed unto them, the said president and fellows of Harvard College, and to their successors, and to their officers and servants, respectively, forever.

Article II.

And whereas there have been at sundry times, by divers persons, gifts, grants, devises of houses, lands, tenements, goods, chattels, legacies and conveyances, heretofore made, either to Harvard College in Cambridge, in New England, or to the president and fellows of Harvard College, or to the said college, by some other description, under several charters successively: it is declared, that all the said gifts, grants, devises, legacies and conveyances, are hereby forever confirmed unto the president and fellows of Harvard College, and to their successors in the capacity aforesaid, according to the true intent and meaning of the donor or donors, grantor or grantors, devisor or devisors.

Article III.

[And whereas, by an act of the general court of the colony of Massachusetts Bay passed in the year one thousand six hundred and forty-two, the governor and deputy-governor, for the time being, and all the magistrates of that jurisdiction, were, with the president, and a number of the clergy in the said act described, constituted the overseers of Harvard College: and it being necessary, in this new constitution of government to ascertain who shall be deemed successors to the said governor, deputy-governor and magistrates; it is declared, that the governor, lieutenant governor, council and senate of this commonwealth, are and shall be deemed, their successors, who with the president of Harvard College, for the time being, together with the ministers of the congregational churches in the towns of Cambridge, Watertown, Charlestown, Boston, Roxbury, and Dorchester, mentioned in the said act, shall be, and hereby are, vested with all the powers and authority belonging, or in any way appertaining to the overseers of Harvard College; provided, that] nothing herein shall be construed to prevent the legislature of this commonwealth from making such alterations in the government of the said university, as shall be conducive to its advantage and the interest of the republic of letters, in as full a manner as might have been done by the legislature of the late Province of the Massachusetts Bay.

Chapter V. Section II: The Encouragement of Literature, etc.

Wisdom, and knowledge, as well as virtue, diffused generally among the body of the people, being necessary for the preservation of their rights and liberties; and as these depend on spreading the opportunities and advantages of education in the various parts of the country, and among the different orders of the people, it shall be the duty of legislatures and magistrates, in all future periods of this commonwealth, to cherish the interests of literature and the sciences, and all seminaries of them; especially the university at Cambridge, public schools and grammar schools in the towns; to encourage private societies and public institutions, rewards and immunities, for the promotion of agriculture, arts, sciences, commerce, trades, manufactures, and a natural history of the country; to countenance and inculcate the principles of humanity and general benevolence, public and private charity, industry and frugality, honesty and punctuality in their dealings; sincerity, good humor, and all social affections, and generous sentiments among the people. [See Amendments, Articles XVIII, XLVI, XCVI and CIII]

Chapter VI, OATHS AND SUBSCRIPTIONS; INCOMPATIBILITY OF AND EXCLUSION FROM OFFICES; PECUNIARY QUALIFICATIONS; COMMISSIONS; WRITS; CONFIRMATION OF LAWS; HABEAS CORPUS; THE ENACTING STYLE; CONTINUANCE OF OFFICERS; PROVISION FOR A FUTURE REVISAL OF THE CONSTITUTION, ETC.

Article I.

[Any person chosen governor, lieutenant governor, councillor, senator or representative, and accepting the trust, shall before he proceed to execute the duties of his place or office, make and subscribe the following declaration, viz.--

"I, A. B., do declare, that I believe the Christian religion, and have a firm persuasion of its truth; and that I am seised and possessed, in my own right, of the property required by the constitution as one qualification for the office or place to which I am elected."

And the governor, lieutenant governor, and councillors shall make and subscribe the said declaration, in the presence of the two houses of assembly; and the senators and representatives first elected under this constitution, before the president and five of the council of the former constitution, and forever afterwards before the governor and council for the time being.]
And every person chosen to either of the places or offices aforesaid, as also any person appointed or commissioned to any judicial, executive, military, or other office under the government, shall, before he enters on the discharge of the business of his place or office, take and subscribe the following declaration, and oaths or affirmations, viz.--

["I, A. B., do truly and sincerely acknowledge, profess, testify and declare, that the Commonwealth of Massachusetts is, and of right ought to be, a free, sovereign and independent state; and I do swear, that I will bear true faith and allegiance to the said commonwealth, and that I will defend the same against traitorous conspiracies and all hostile attempts whatsoever: and that I do renounce and abjure all allegiance, subjection and obedience to the king, queen, or government of Great Britain, (as the case may be) and every other foreign power whatsoever: and that no foreign prince, person, prelate, state or potentate, hath, or ought to have, any jurisdiction, superiority, pre-eminence, authority, dispensing or other power, in any matter, civil, ecclesiastical or spiritual, within this commonwealth, except the authority and power which is or may be vested by their constituents in the congress of the United States: and I do further testify and declare, that no man or body of men hath or can have any right to absolve or discharge me from the obligation of this oath, declaration, or affirmation; and that I do make this acknowledgment, profession, testimony, declaration, denial, renunciation and abjuration, heartily and truly, according to the common meaning and acceptation of the foregoing words, without any equivocation, mental evasion, or secret reservation whatsoever -- So help me, God."]

"I, A. B., do solemnly swear and affirm, that I will faithfully and impartially discharge and perform all the duties incumbent on me as : according to the best of my abilities and understanding, agreeably, to the rules and regulations of the constitution, and the laws of this commonwealth -- So help me, God."
Provided always, that when any person chosen or appointed as aforesaid, shall be of the denomination of the people called Quakers, and shall decline taking the said oath[s], he shall make his affirmation in the foregoing form, and subscribe the same, omitting the words:

["I do swear," "and abjure," "oath or," "and abjuration" in the first oath; and in the second oath, the words] "swear and," and [in each of them] the words "So help me, God;" subjoining instead thereof, "This I do under the pains and penalties of perjury."] [See Amendments, Article VI]

And the said oaths or affirmations shall be taken and subscribed by the governor, lieutenant governor, and councillors, before the president of the senate, in the presence of the two houses of assembly; and by the senators and representatives first elected under this constitution, before the president and five of the council of the former constitution; and forever afterwards before the governor and council for the time being: and by the residue of the officers aforesaid, before such persons and in such manner as from time to time shall be prescribed by the legislature. [See Amendments, Articles VI and VII]

Article II.

No governor, lieutenant governor, or judge of the supreme judicial court, shall hold any other office or place, under the authority of this commonwealth, except such as by this constitution they are admitted to hold saving that the judges of the said court may hold the offices of justices of the peace through the state; nor shall they hold any other place or office, or receive any pension or salary from any other state or government or power whatever.

No person shall be capable of holding or exercising at the same time, within this state more than one of the following offices, viz. -- judge of probate -- sheriff -- register of probate -- or register of deeds -- and never more than any two offices which are to be held by appointment of the governor, or the governor and council, or the senate, or the house of representatives, or by the election of the people of the state at large, or of the people of any county, military offices and the offices of justices of the peace excepted, shall be held by one person.

No person holding the office of judge of the supreme judicial court -- secretary -- attorney-general -- solicitor-general -- treasurer or receiver-general -- judge of probate -- commissary-general -- [president, professor, or instructor of Harvard College] -- sheriff -- clerk of the house of representatives -- register of probate -- register of deeds -- clerk of the supreme judicial court -- clerk of the inferior court of common pleas -- or officer of the customs, including in this description naval officers -- shall at the same time have a seat in the senate or house of representatives; but their being chosen or appointed to, and accepting the same, shall operate as a resignation of their seat in the senate or house of representatives; and the place so vacated shall be filled up. [See Amendments, Articles VIII and XXVII]

And the same rule shall take place in case any judge of the said supreme judicial court, or judge of probate, shall accept a seat in council; or any councillor shall accept of either of those offices or places.

And no person shall ever be admitted to hold a seat in the legislature, or any office of trust or importance under the government of this commonwealth, who shall, in the due course of law, have been convicted of bribery or corruption in obtaining an election or appointment. [See Amendments, Article LXV]

Article III.

[In all cases where sums of money are mentioned in this constitution, the value thereof shall be computed in silver at six shillings and eight pence per ounce: and it shall be in the power of the legislature, from time to time, to increase such qualifications, as to property, of the persons to be elected to offices, as the circumstances of the commonwealth shall require.] [See Amendments, Articles XIII and XXXIV]

Article IV.

All commissions shall be in the name of the Commonwealth of Massachusetts, signed by the governor and attested by the secretary or his deputy, and have the great seal of the commonwealth affixed thereto.

Article V.

All writs issuing out of the clerk's office in any of the courts of law, shall be in the name of the Commonwealth of Massachusetts: they shall be under the seal of the court from whence they issue: they shall bear test of the first justice of the court to which they shall be returnable, who is not a party, and be signed by the clerk of such court.

Article VI.

All the laws which have heretofore been adopted, used and approved in the Province, Colony or State of Massachusetts Bay, and usually practiced on in the courts of law, shall still remain and be in full force, until altered or repealed by the legislature; such parts only excepted as are repugnant to the rights and liberties contained in this constitution.

Article VII.

The privilege and benefit of the writ of habeas corpus shall be enjoyed in this commonwealth in the most free, easy, cheap, expeditious and ample manner; and shall not be suspended by the legislature, except upon the most urgent and pressing occasions, and for a limited time not exceeding twelve months.

Article VIII.

The enacting style, in making and passing all acts, statutes and laws, shall be -- "Be it enacted by the Senate and House of Representatives in General Court assembled, and by the authority of the same."

Article IX.

[To the end there may be no failure of justice, or danger arise to the commonwealth from a change of the form of government -- all officers, civil and military, holding commissions under the government and people of Massachusetts Bay in New England, and all other officers of the said government and people, at the time this constitution shall take effect, shall have, hold, use, exercise and enjoy, all the powers and authority to them granted or committed, until other persons shall be appointed in their stead: and all courts of law shall proceed in the execution of the business of their respective departments; and all the executive and legislative officers, bodies and powers shall continue in full force, in the enjoyment and exercise of all their trusts, employments and authority; until the general court and the supreme and executive officers under this constitution are designated and invested with their respective trusts powers and authority.]

Article X.

[In order the more effectually to adhere to the principles of the constitution, and to correct those violations which by any means may be made therein, as well as to form such alterations as from experience shall be found necessary -- the general court which shall be in the year of our Lord one thousand seven hundred and ninety-five, shall issue precepts to the selectmen of the several towns, and to the assessors of the unincorporated plantations, directing them to convene the qualified voters of their respective towns and plantations, for the purpose of collecting their sentiments on the necessity or expediency of revising the constitution, in order to amendments. [See Amendments, Article IX]

And if it shall appear by the returns made, that two thirds of the qualified voters throughout the state, who shall assemble and vote in consequence of the said precepts, are in favor of such revision or amendment, the general court shall issue precepts, or direct them to be issued from the secretary's office to the several towns to elect delegates to meet in convention for the purpose aforesaid.

The said delegates to be chosen in the same manner and proportion as their representatives in the second branch of the legislature are by this constitution to be chosen.] [Annulled by Amendments, Article XLVIII]

Article XI.

This form of government shall be enrolled on parchment and deposited in the secretary's office, and be a part of the laws of the land -- and printed copies thereof shall be prefixed to the book containing the laws of this commonwealth, in all future editions of the said laws.

ARTICLES OF AMENDMENT

Article I.

[If any bill or resolve shall be objected to, and not approved by the governor; and if the general court shall adjourn within five days after the same shall have been laid before the governor for his approbation, and thereby prevent his returning it with his objections, as provided by the constitution, such bill or resolve shall not become a law, nor have force as such.] [See Constitution, Chapter 1, Section 1, Article II] [Superseded by Amendments, Article XC, Section 2]

Article II.

[The general court shall have full power and authority to erect and constitute municipal or city governments, in any corporate town or towns in this commonwealth, and to grant to the inhabitants thereof such powers, privileges, and immunities, not repugnant to the constitution as the general court shall deem necessary or expedient for the regulation and government thereof and to prescribe the manner of calling and holding public meetings of the inhabitants, in wards or otherwise for the election of officers under the constitution, and the manner of returning the votes given at such meetings. Provided, that no such government shall be erected or constituted in any town not containing twelve thousand inhabitants, nor unless it be with the consent, and on the application of a majority of the inhabitants of such town, present and voting thereon, pursuant to a vote at a meeting duly warned and holden for that purpose. And provided also, that all by-laws made by such municipal or city government shall be subject, at all times to be annulled by the general court.] [See Amendments, Article LXX] [Annulled by Amendments, Article LXXXIX]

Article III.

Every [male] citizen of [twenty-one] years of age and upwards, excepting [paupers and] persons under guardianship who shall have resided [within the commonwealth one year, and] within the town or district in which he may claim a right to vote, six calendar months next preceding any election of governor, lieutenant governor, senators, or representatives, [and who shall have paid, by himself or his parent, master or guardian, any state or county tax, which shall, within two years next preceding such election, have been assessed upon him in any town or district of this commonwealth; and also, every citizen who shall be, by law, exempted from taxation, and who shall be, in all other respects, qualified as above mentioned,] shall have a right to vote in such election of governor, lieutenant governor, senators and representatives; and no other person shall be entitled to vote in such election. [See Amendments, Articles XX, XXIII, XXVI, XXVIII, XXX, XXXI, XXXII, XL, LXVIII, LXIX, XCIII, XCIV, XCV, and C] [For absent voting, see Amendments, Articles XLV and LXXVI]

Article IV.

Notaries public shall be appointed by the governor in the same manner as judicial officers are appointed, and shall hold their offices during seven years, unless sooner removed by the governor with the consent of the council, upon the address of both houses of the legislature. [See Amendments, Articles XXXVII, LXII, and LXIX, section 2]

[In case the office of secretary or treasurer of the commonwealth shall become vacant from any cause during the recess of the general court, the governor, with the advice and consent of the council, shall nominate and appoint, under such regulations as may be prescribed by law, a competent and suitable person to such vacant office, who shall hold the same until a successor shall be appointed by the general court.] [This paragraph superseded by Amendments, Article XVII]

[Whenever the exigencies of the commonwealth shall require the appointment of a commissary-general, he shall be nominated, appointed and commissioned in such manner as the legislature may, by law, prescribe.

All officers commissioned to command in the militia may be removed from office in such manner as the legislature may, by law, prescribe.] [Last two paragraphs annulled and superseded by Amendments, Article LIII]

Article V.

[In the elections of captains and subalterns of the militia, all the members of their respective companies, as well those under as those above the age of twenty-one years, shall have a right to vote.] [Annulled by Amendments, Article LIII]

Article VI.

Instead of the oath of allegiance prescribed by the constitution, the following oath shall be taken and subscribed by every person chosen or appointed to any office, civil or military under the government of this commonwealth, before he shall enter on the duties of his office, to wit:

"I, A. B. do solemnly swear, that I will bear true faith and allegiance to the Commonwealth of Massachusetts, and will support the constitution thereof. So help me God."

Provided, That when any person shall be of the denomination called Quakers, and shall decline taking said oath, he shall make his affirmation in the foregoing form, omitting the word "swear" and inserting instead thereof the word "affirm;" and omitting the words "So help me God," and subjoining, instead thereof, the words "This I do under the pains and penalties of perjury." [see Constitution, Chapter VI, Article I]

Article VII.

No oath, declaration or subscription, excepting the oath prescribed in the preceding article and the oath of office, shall be required of the governor, lieutenant governor, councillors, senators or representatives, to qualify them to perform the duties of their respective offices.

Article VIII.

No judge of any court of this commonwealth (except the court of sessions) and no person holding any office under the authority of the United States (postmasters excepted) shall, at the same time, hold the office of governor, lieutenant governor, or councillor, or have a seat in the senate or house of representatives of this commonwealth; and no judge of any court in this commonwealth (except the court of sessions) nor the attorney-general, solicitor-general, county attorney, clerk of any court, sheriff, treasurer and receiver-general, register of probate, nor register of deeds, shall continue to hold his said office after being elected a member of Congress of the United States, and accepting that trust; but the acceptance of such trust by any of the officers aforesaid shall be deemed and taken to be a resignation of his said office; and judges of the courts of common pleas shall hold no other office under the government of this commonwealth, the office of justice of the peace and militia offices excepted. [See Amendments, Article LXV]

Article IX.

[If, at any time hereafter, any specific and particular amendment or amendments to the constitution be proposed in the general court, and agreed to by a majority of the senators and two thirds of the members of the house of representatives present and voting thereon, such proposed amendment or amendments shall be entered on the journals of the two houses, with the yeas and nays taken thereon, and referred to the general court then next to be chosen, and shall be published; and if, in the general court next chosen as aforesaid, such proposed amendment or amendments shall be agreed to by a majority of the senators and two thirds of the members of the house of representatives present and voting thereon; then it shall be the duty of the general court to submit such proposed amendment or amendments to the people: and if they shall be approved and ratified by a majority of the qualified voters voting thereon, at meetings legally warned and holden for that purpose, they shall become part of the constitution of this commonwealth.] [Annulled by Amendments, Article XLVIII, General Provisions, VIII]

Article X.

The political year shall begin on the first Wednesday of January instead of the last Wednesday of May, and the general court shall assemble every year on the said first Wednesday of January, and shall proceed at that session to make all the elections, and do all the other acts which are by the constitution required to be made and done at the session which has heretofore commenced on the last Wednesday of May. And the general court shall be dissolved on the next day preceding the first Wednesday of January, without any proclamation or other act of the governor. But nothing herein contained shall prevent the general court from assembling at such other times as they shall judge necessary, or when called together by the governor. [The governor, lieutenant governor and councillors, shall also hold their respective offices for one year next following the first Wednesday of January, and until others are chosen and qualified in their stead.] [See Amendments, Articles XIV, LXXII, and LXXV]

[The meeting for the choice of governor, lieutenant governor, senators and representatives shall be held on the second Monday of November in every year; but meetings may be adjourned if necessary, for the choice of representatives, to the next day, and again to the next succeeding day, but no further. But in case a second meeting shall be necessary for the choice of representatives, such meetings shall be held on the fourth Monday of the same month of November.] [See Amendments, Article LXIV] [This paragraph superseded by Amendments, Article XV]

All the other provisions of the constitution, respecting the elections and proceedings of the members of the general court, or of any other officers or persons whatever, that have reference to the last Wednesday of May, as the commencement of the political year, shall be so far altered as to have like reference to the first Wednesday of January.

This article shall go into operation on the first day of October next following the day when the same shall be duly ratified and adopted as an amendment of the constitution[; -- and the governor, lieutenant governor, councillors, senators, representatives and all other state officers, who are annually chosen, and who shall be chosen for the current year when the same shall go into operation, shall hold their respective offices until the first Wednesday of January then next following, and until others are chosen and qualified in their stead, and no longer -- and the first election of the governor, lieutenant governor, senators and representatives to be had in virtue of this article shall be had conformably thereunto, in the month of November following the day on which the same shall be in force, and go into operation pursuant to the foregoing provision.]
All the provisions of the existing constitution inconsistent with the provisions herein contained are hereby wholly annulled. [See Amendments, Article LXIV]

Article XI.

Instead of the third article of the bill of rights, the following modification and amendment thereof is substituted.

"As the public worship of God and instructions in piety, religion and morality, promote the happiness and prosperity of a people and the security of a republican government; -- therefore, the several religious societies of this commonwealth, whether corporate or unincorporate, at any meeting legally warned and holden for that purpose, shall ever have the right to elect their pastors or religious teachers, to contract with them for their support, to raise money for erecting and repairing houses for public worship, for the maintenance of religious instruction, and for the payment of necessary expenses: and all persons belonging to any religious society shall be taken and held to be members, until they shall file with the clerk of such society, a written notice, declaring the dissolution of their membership, and thenceforth shall not be liable for any grant or contract which may be thereafter made, or entered into by such society: -- and all religious sects and denominations, demeaning themselves peaceably, and as good citizens of the commonwealth, shall be equally under the protection of the law; and no subordination of any one sect or denomination to another shall ever be established by law." [See Amendments, Articles XLVI and XLVIII, The Initiative, section 2, and The Referendum, section 2]

Article XII.

[In order to provide for a representation of the citizens of this commonwealth, founded upon the principles of equality a census of the ratable polls, in each city, town and district of the commonwealth, on the first day of May, shall be taken and returned into the secretary's office, in such manner as the legislature shall provide, within the month of May, in the year of our Lord one thousand eight hundred and thirty-seven, and in every tenth year thereafter, in the month of May, in manner aforesaid, and each town or city having three hundred ratable polls at the last preceding decennial census of polls may elect one representative, and for every four hundred and fifty ratable polls in addition to the first three hundred, one representative more.

Any town having less then three hundred ratable polls shall be represented thus; the whole number of ratable polls, at the last preceding decennial census of polls, shall be multiplied by ten, and the product divided by three hundred, and such town may elect one representative as many years within ten years, as three hundred is contained in the product aforesaid.

Any city or town having ratable polls enough to elect one or more representatives, with any number of polls beyond the necessary number, may be represented as to that surplus number by multiplying such surplus number by ten and dividing the product by four hundred and fifty; and such city or town may elect one additional representative as many years within the ten years as four hundred and fifty is contained in the product aforesaid.

Any two or more of the several towns and districts may, by consent of a majority of the legal voters present at a legal meeting in each of said towns and districts respectively called for that purpose, and held previous to the first day of July in the year in which the decennial census of polls shall be taken, form themselves into a representative district, to continue until the next decennial census of polls, for the election of a representative or representatives, and such district shall have all the rights, in regard to representation, which would belong to a town containing the same number of ratable polls.

The governor and council shall ascertain and determine within the months of July and August, in the year of our Lord one thousand eight hundred and thirty-seven, according to the foregoing principles, the number of representatives, which each city, town and representative district is entitled to elect, and the number of years within the period of ten years then next ensuing, that each city, town and representative district may elect an additional representative, and where any town has not a sufficient number of polls to elect a representative each year then how many years within the ten years, such town may elect a representative, and the same shall be done once in ten years thereafter by the governor and council, and the number of ratable polls in each decennial census of polls, shall determine the number of representatives, which each city, town and representative district may elect as aforesaid, and when the number of representatives to be elected by each city, town or representative district is ascertained and determined as aforesaid, the governor shall cause the same to be published forthwith for the information of the people and that number shall remain fixed and unalterable for the period of ten years.
All the provisions of the existing constitution inconsistent with the provisions herein contained, are hereby wholly annulled.]
[Superseded by Amendments, Articles XIII, XXI, LXXI, XCII, CI and, XXI, LXXI, XCII, CI and CIX]

Article XIII.

[A census of the inhabitants of each city and town, on the first day of May, shall be taken, and returned into the secretary's office, on or before the last day of June, of the year one thousand eight hundred and forty, and of every tenth year thereafter, which census shall determine the apportionment of senators and representatives for the term of ten years. [See Amendments, Articles XXI, XXII LXXI, XCII, CI and CIX]

The several senatorial districts now existing shall be permanent. The senate shall consist of forty members: and in the year one thousand eight hundred and forty, and every tenth year thereafter, the governor and council shall assign the number of senators to be chosen in each district, according to the number of inhabitants in the same. But, in all cases, at least one senator shall be assigned to each district. [See Amendments, Articles XXII, LXXI, XCII, CI and CIX]

The members of the house of representatives shall be apportioned in the following manner: Every town or city containing twelve hundred inhabitants, may elect one representative; and two thousand four hundred inhabitants shall be the mean increasing number which shall entitle it to an additional representative. [See Amendments, Articles XXI, XXII LXXI, XCII, CI and CIX]

Every town containing less than twelve hundred inhabitants, shall be entitled to elect a representative as many times, within ten years, as the number one hundred and sixty is contained in the number of the inhabitants of said town. Such towns may also elect one representative for the year in which the valuation of estates within the commonwealth shall be settled.

Any two or more of the several towns may, by consent of a majority of the legal voters present at a legal meeting, in each of said towns respectively, called for that purpose, and held before the first day of August, in the year one thousand eight hundred and forty, and every tenth year thereafter, form themselves into a representative district, to continue for the term of ten years; and such district shall have all the rights in regard to representation, which would belong to a town containing the same number of inhabitants

The number of inhabitants which shall entitle a town to elect one representative, and the mean increasing number, which shall entitle a town or city to elect more than one, and also the number by which the population of towns, not entitled to a representative every year, is to be divided, shall be increased respectively, by one tenth of the numbers above mentioned, whenever the population of the commonwealth shall have increased to seven hundred and seventy thousand, and for every additional increase of seventy thousand inhabitants, the same addition of one tenth shall be made, respectively, to the said numbers above mentioned.

In the year of each decennial census, the governor and council shall, before the first day of September, apportion the number of representatives which each city, town, and representative district is entitled to elect, and ascertain how many years within ten years, any town may elect a representative, which is not entitled to elect one every year; and the governor shall cause the same to be published forthwith.

Nine councillors shall be annually chosen from among the people at large, on the first Wednesday of January, or as soon thereafter as may be, by the joint ballot of the senators and representatives assembled in one room, who shall, as soon as may be, in like manner, fill up any vacancies that may happen in the council, by death, resignation, or otherwise. No person shall be elected a councillor, who has not been an inhabitant of this commonwealth for the term of five years immediately preceding his election; and not more than one councillor shall be chosen from any one senatorial district in the commonwealth.] [See Amendments, Articles XVI, LXIV, LXXX, XCII, CI and CIX]

No possession of a freehold or of any other estate shall be required as a qualification for holding a seat in either branch of the general court, or in the executive council.

Article XIV.

In all elections of civil officers by the people of this commonwealth, whose election is provided for by the constitution, the person having the highest number of votes shall be deemed and declared to be elected.

Article XV.

[The meeting for the choice of governor, lieutenant-governor, senators and representatives, shall be held on the Tuesday next after the first Monday in November, annually; but in case of a failure to elect representatives on that day, a second meeting shall be holden for that purpose on the fourth Monday of the same month of November.] [See Amendments, Articles LXIV and LXXX]

Article XVI.

Eight councillors shall be annually chosen by the inhabitants of this commonwealth, qualified to vote for governor. The election of councillors shall be determined by the same rule that is required in the election of governor. The legislature, at its first session after this amendment shall have been adopted, and at its first session after the next state census shall have been taken, and at its first session after each decennial state census thereafterwards, shall divide the commonwealth into eight districts of contiguous territory, each containing a number of inhabitants as nearly equal as practicable, without dividing any town or ward of a city, and each entitled to elect one councillor: provided, however, that if, at any time, the constitution shall provide for the division of the commonwealth into forty senatorial districts, then the legislature shall so arrange the councillor districts that each district shall consist of five contiguous senatorial districts, as they shall be, from time to time, established by the legislature. No person shall be eligible to the office of councillor who has not been an inhabitant of the commonwealth for the term of five years immediately preceding his election. The day and manner of the election, the return of the votes, and the declaration of the said elections, shall be the same as are required in the election of governor. [Whenever there shall be a failure to elect the full number of councillors, the vacancies shall be filled in the same manner as is required for filling vacancies in the senate; and vacancies occasioned by death, removal from the state, or otherwise, shall be filled in like manner, as soon as may be after such vacancies shall have happened.] And that there may be no delay in the organization of the government on the first Wednesday of January, the governor, with at least five councillors for the time being, shall, as soon as may be, examine the returned copies of the records for the election of governor, lieutenant-governor, and councillors; and ten days before the said first Wednesday in January he shall issue his summons to such persons as appear to be chosen, to attend on that day to be qualified accordingly; and the secretary shall lay the returns before the senate and house of representatives on the said first Wednesday in January, to be by them examined; and in case of the election of either of said officers, the choice shall be by them declared and published; but in case there shall be no election of either of said officers, the legislature shall proceed to fill such vacancies in the manner provided in the constitution for the choice of such officers. [See Amendments, ArtsXXV, LXIV and LXXX]

Article XVII.

The secretary, treasurer and receiver-general, auditor, and attorney-general, shall be chosen [annually,] on the day in November prescribed for the choice of governor; and each person then chosen as such, duly qualified in other respects, shall hold his office for the term of [one year] from the third Wednesday in January next thereafter, and until another is chosen and qualified in his stead. The qualification of the voters, the manner of the election, the return of the votes, and the declaration of the election, shall be such as are required in the election of governor. In case of a failure to elect either of said officers on the day in November aforesaid, or in case of the decease in the mean time of the person elected as such, such officer shall be chosen on or before the third Wednesday in January next thereafter from the [two persons who had the highest number of votes for said offices on the day in November aforesaid], by joint ballot of the senators and representatives in one room; and in case the office of secretary, or treasurer and receiver-general, or auditor, or attorney-general, shall become vacant from any cause during an annual or special session of the general court, such vacancy shall in like manner be filled by choice from the people at large; but if such vacancy shall occur at any other time, it shall be supplied by the governor by appointment, with the advice and consent of the council. The person so chosen or appointed, duly qualified in other respects, shall hold his office until his successor is chosen and duly qualified in his stead. In case any person chosen or appointed to either of the offices aforesaid, shall neglect, for the space of ten days after he could otherwise enter upon his duties, to qualify himself in all respects to enter upon the discharge of such duties, the office to which he has been elected or appointed shall be deemed vacant. No person shall be eligible to either of said offices unless he shall have been an inhabitant of this commonwealth five years next preceding his election or appointment. [See Amendments, Articles LXIV, LXXIX and LXXX]

Article XVIII.

[All moneys raised by taxation in the towns and cities for the support of public schools, and all moneys which may be appropriated by the state for the support of common schools, shall be applied to, and expended in, no other schools than those which are conducted according to law, under the order and superintendence of the authorities of the town or city in which the money is to be expended; and such moneys shall never be appropriated to any religious sect for the maintenance exclusively of its own schools.] [Superseded by Amendments, Articles XLVI, XCVI and CIII]

Article XIX.

The legislature shall prescribe, by general law, for the election of sheriffs, registers of probate, [commissioners of insolvency,] and clerks of the courts, by the people of the several counties, and that district-attorneys shall be chosen by the people of the several districts, for such term of office as the legislature shall prescribe. [See Amendments, Article XXXVI]

Article XX.

No person shall [have the right to vote, or] be eligible to office under the constitution of this commonwealth, who shall not be able to read the constitution in the English language, and write his name: -- provided, however, that the provisions of this amendment shall not apply to any person prevented by a physical disability from complying with its requisitions, nor to any person who now has the right to vote, nor to any persons who shall be sixty years of age or upwards at the time this amendment shall take effect. [See Amendments, Articles III, XXIII, XXVI, XXVIII, XXX, XXXI, XXXII, XL, XLV and LXXVI]

Article XXI.

[A census of the legal voters of each city and town, on the first day of May, shall be taken and returned into the office of the secretary of the commonwealth, on or before the last day of June, in the year one thousand eight hundred and fifty-seven; and a census of the inhabitants of each city and town, in the year one thousand eight hundred and sixty-five, and of every tenth year thereafter. In the census aforesaid, a special enumeration shall be made of the legal voters; and in each city, said enumeration shall specify the number of such legal voters aforesaid, residing in each ward of such city. The enumeration aforesaid shall determine the apportionment of representatives for the periods between the taking of the census.

The house of representatives shall consist of two hundred and forty members, which shall be apportioned, by the legislature, at its first session after the return of each enumeration as aforesaid, to the several counties of the commonwealth, equally, as nearly as may be, according to their relative numbers of legal voters, as ascertained by the next preceding special enumeration; and the town of Cohasset, in the county of Norfolk, shall, for this purpose, as well as in the formation of districts, as hereinafter provided, be considered as part of the county of Plymouth; and it shall be the duty of the secretary of the commonwealth, to certify, as soon as may be after it is determined by the legislature, the number of representatives to which each county shall be entitled, to the board authorized to divide each county into representative districts. The mayor and aldermen of the city of Boston, the county commissioners of other counties than Suffolk, -- or in lieu of the mayor and aldermen of the city of Boston, or of the county commissioners in each county other than Suffolk, such board of special commissioners in each county, to be elected by the people of the county, or of the towns therein, as may for that purpose be provided by law, shall, on the first Tuesday of August next after each assignment of representatives to each county, assemble at a shire town of their respective counties, and proceed, as soon as may be, to divide the same into representative districts of contiguous territory, so as to apportion the representation assigned to each county equally, as nearly as may be, according to the relative number of legal voters in the several districts of each county; and such districts shall be so formed that no town or ward of a city shall be divided therefor, nor shall any district be made which shall be entitled to elect more than three representatives. Every representative, for one year at least next preceding his election, shall have been an inhabitant of the district for which he is chosen, and shall cease to represent such district when he shall cease to be an inhabitant of the commonwealth. The districts in each county shall be numbered by the board creating the same, and a description of each, with the numbers thereof and the number of legal voters therein, shall be returned by the board, to the secretary of the commonwealth, the county treasurer of each county, and to the clerk of every town in each district, to be filed and kept in their respective offices. The manner of calling and conducting the meetings for the choice of representatives, and of ascertaining their election, shall be prescribed by law.] [Not less than one hundred members of the house of representatives shall constitute a quorum for doing business; but a less number may organize temporarily, adjourn from day to day, and compel the attendance of absent members.] [Annulled and superseded by Amendments, Articles XXXIII, LXXI, CI, and CIX]

Article XXII.

[A census of the legal voters of each city and town, on the first day of May, shall be taken and returned into the office of the secretary of the commonwealth, on or before the last day of June, in the year one thousand eight hundred and fifty-seven; and a census of the inhabitants of each city and town, in the year one thousand eight hundred and sixty-five, and of every tenth year thereafter. In the census aforesaid, a special enumeration shall be made of the legal voters, and in each city said enumeration shall specify the number of such legal voters aforesaid, residing in each ward of such city. The enumeration aforesaid shall determine the apportionment of senators for the periods between the taking of the census. The senate shall consist of forty members. The general court shall, at its first session after each next preceding special enumeration, divide the commonwealth into forty districts of adjacent territory, each district to contain, as nearly as may be, an equal number of legal voters, according to the enumeration aforesaid: -- provided, however, no town or ward of a city shall be divided therefor; and such districts shall be formed, as nearly as may be, without uniting two counties, or parts of two or more counties, into one district. Each district shall elect one senator, who shall have been an inhabitant of this commonwealth five years at least immediately preceding his election, and at the time of his election shall be an inhabitant of the district for which he is chosen; and he shall cease to represent such senatorial district when he shall cease to be an inhabitant of the commonwealth.] [Not less than sixteen senators shall constitute a quorum for doing business; but a less number may organize temporarily, adjourn from day to day, and compel the attendance of absent members.] [See Amendments, Article XXIV] [Annulled and superseded by Amendments, Articles XXXIII, LXXI, XCII, CI and CIX]

Article XXIII.

[No person of foreign birth shall be entitled to vote, or shall be eligible to office, unless he shall have resided within the jurisdiction of the United States for two years subsequent to his naturalization, and shall be otherwise qualified, according to the constitution and laws of this commonwealth: provided, that this amendment shall not affect the rights which any person of foreign birth possessed at the time of the adoption thereof; and, provided, further, that it shall not affect the rights of any child of a citizen of the United States, born during the temporary absence of the parent therefrom.] [Annulled by Amendments, Article XXVI]

Article XXIV.

Any vacancy in the senate shall be filled by election by the people of the unrepresented district, upon the order of a majority of senators elected.

Article XXV.

In case of a vacancy in the council, from a failure of election or other cause, the senate and house of representatives shall, by concurrent vote, choose some eligible person from the people of the district wherein such vacancy occurs, to fill that office. If such vacancy shall happen when the legislature is not in session, the governor, with the advice and consent of the council, may fill the same by appointment of some eligible person.

Article XXVI.

The twenty-third article of the articles of amendment of the constitution of this commonwealth, which is as follows, to wit: -- "No person of foreign birth shall be entitled to vote, or shall be eligible to office, unless he shall have resided within the jurisdiction of the United States, for two years subsequent to his naturalization, and shall be otherwise qualified according to the constitution and laws of this commonwealth: provided, that this amendment shall not affect the rights which any person of foreign birth possessed at the time of the adoption thereof; and provided, further, that it shall not affect the rights of any child of a citizen of the United States, born during the temporary absence of the parent therefrom," is hereby wholly annulled.

Article XXVII.

So much of article two of chapter six of the constitution of this commonwealth as relates to persons holding the office of president, professor or instructor of Harvard College is hereby annulled.

Article XXVIII.

No person having served in the army or navy of the United States in time of war, and having been honorably discharged from such service, if otherwise qualified to vote, shall be disqualified therefor on account of [being a pauper;] or, [if a pauper,] because of the non-payment of a poll tax.] [Amended by Amendments, Article XXXI]

Article XXIX.

The general court shall have full power and authority to provide for the inhabitants of the towns in this commonwealth more than one place of public meeting within the limits of each town for the election of officers under the constitution, and to prescribe the manner of calling, holding and conducting such meetings. All the provisions of the existing constitution inconsistent with the provisions herein contained are hereby annulled. [For absent voting, see Amendments, Articles XLV and LXXVI]

Article XXX.

No person, otherwise qualified to vote in elections for governor, lieutenant-governor, senators, and representatives, shall, by reason of a change of residence within the commonwealth, be disqualified from voting for said officers in the city or town from which he has removed his residence, until the expiration of six calendar months from the time of such removal. [For absent and compulsory voting, see Amendments, Articles XLV, LXI and LXXVI]

Article XXXI.

[Article twenty-eight of the amendments of the constitution is hereby amended by striking out in the fourth line thereof the words "being a pauper", and inserting in place thereof the words: -- receiving or having received aid from any city or town, -- and also by striking out in said fourth line the words "if a pauper", so that the article as amended shall read as follows:

ARTICLE XXVIII. No person having served in the army or navy of the United States in time of war, and having been honorably discharged from such service, if otherwise qualified to vote, shall be disqualified therefor on account of receiving or having received aid from any city or town, or because of the non-payment of a poll tax.]

Article XXXII.

So much of article three of the amendments of the constitution of the commonwealth as is contained in the following words: "and who shall have paid, by himself, or his parent, master, or guardian, any state or county tax, which shall, within two years next preceding such election, have been assessed upon him, in any town or district of this commonwealth; and also every citizen who shall be, by law, exempted from taxation, and who shall be, in all other respects, qualified as above mentioned", is hereby annulled.

Article XXXIII.

A majority of the members of each branch of the general court shall constitute a quorum for the transaction of business, but a less number may adjourn from day to day, and compel the attendance of absent members. All the provisions of the existing constitution inconsistent with the provisions herein contained are hereby annulled.

Article XXXIV.

So much of article two of section one of chapter two of part the second of the constitution of the commonwealth as is contained in the following words: "and unless he shall at the same time, be seised in his own right, of a freehold within the commonwealth of the value of one thousand pounds"; is hereby annulled.

Article XXXV.

So much of article two of section three of chapter one of the constitution of the commonwealth as is contained in the following words: "The expenses of travelling to the general assembly, and returning home, once in every session, and no more, shall be paid by the government, out of the public treasury, to every member who shall attend as seasonably as he can, in the judgment of the house, and does not depart without leave", is hereby annulled.

Article XXXVI.

So much of article nineteen of the articles of amendment to the constitution of the commonwealth as is contained in the following words "commissioners of insolvency", is hereby annulled.

Article XXXVII.

The governor, with the consent of the council, may remove justices of the peace and notaries public.

Article XXXVIII.

Voting machines or other mechanical devices for voting may be used at all elections under such regulations as may be prescribed by law: provided, however, that the right of secret voting shall be preserved.

Article XXXIX.

Article ten of part one of the constitution is hereby amended by adding to it the following words: -- The legislature may by special acts for the purpose of laying out, widening or relocating highways or streets, authorize the taking in fee by the commonwealth, or by a county, city or town, of more land and property than are needed for the actual construction of such highway or street:provided, however, that the land and property authorized to be taken are specified in the act and are no more in extent than would be sufficient for suitable building lots on both sides of such highway or street, and after so much of the land or property has been appropriated for such highway or street as is needed therefor, may authorize the sale of the remainder for value with or without suitable restrictions.

Article XL.

Article three of the amendments to the constitution is hereby amended by inserting after the word "guardianship", in line two, the following: -- and persons temporarily or permanently disqualified by law because of corrupt practices in respect to elections.

Article XLI.

[Full power and authority are hereby given and granted to the general court to prescribe for wild or forest lands such methods of taxation as will develop and conserve the forest resources of the commonwealth.] [Annulled by Amendments, Article CX]

Article XLII.

[Full power and authority are hereby given and granted to the general court to refer to the people for their rejection or approval at the polls any act or resolve of the general court or any part or parts thereof. Such reference shall be by a majority yea and nay vote of all members of each house present and voting. Any act, resolve, or part thereof so referred shall be voted on at the regular state election next ensuing after such reference, shall become law if approved by a majority of the voters voting thereon, and shall take effect at the expiration of thirty days after the election at which it was approved or at such time after the expiration of the said thirty days as may be fixed in such act, resolve or part thereof.] [Annulled and superseded by Amendments, Article XLVIII, General Provisions, VIII]

Article XLIII.

The general court shall have power to authorize the commonwealth to take land and to hold, improve, sub-divide, build upon and sell the same, for the purpose of relieving congestion of population and providing homes for citizens; provided, however, that this amendment shall not be deemed to authorize the sale of such land or buildings at less than the cost thereof.

Article XLIV.

Full power and authority are hereby given and granted to the general court to impose and levy a tax on income in the manner hereinafter provided. Such tax may be at different rates upon income derived from different classes of property, but shall be levied at a uniform rate throughout the commonwealth upon incomes derived from the same class of property. The general court may tax income not derived from property at a lower rate than income derived from property, and may grant reasonable exemptions and abatements. Any class of property the income from which is taxed under the provisions of this article may be exempted from the imposition and levying of proportional and reasonable assessments, rates and taxes as at present authorized by the constitution. This article shall not be construed to limit the power of the general court to impose and levy reasonable duties and excises.

Article XLV.

[The general court shall have power to provide by law for voting by qualified voters of the commonwealth who, at the time of an election, are absent from the city or town of which they are inhabitants in the choice of any officer to be elected or upon any question submitted at such election.] [Annulled and superseded by Amendments, Articles LXXVI and CV] [For compulsory voting, see Amendments, Article LXI]

Article XLVI.

(In place of article XVIII of the articles of amendment of the constitution ratified and adopted April 9, 1821, the following article of amendment, submitted by the constitutional convention, was ratified and adopted November 6, 1917.)

Article XVIII.

Section 1. No law shall be passed prohibiting the free exercise of religion.

Section 2. All moneys raised by taxation in the towns and cities for the support of public schools, and all moneys which may be appropriated by the commonwealth for the support of common schools shall be applied to, and expended in, no other schools than those which are conducted according to law, under the order and superintendence of the authorities of the town or city in which the money is expended; and no grant, appropriation or use of public money or property or loan of public credit shall be made or authorized by the commonwealth or any political division thereof for the purpose of founding, maintaining or aiding any other school or institution of learning, whether under public control or otherwise, wherein any denominational doctrine is inculcated, or any other school, or any college, infirmary, hospital, institution, or educational, charitable or religious undertaking which is not publicly owned and under the exclusive control, order and superintendence of public officers or public agents authorized by the commonwealth or federal authority or both, except that appropriations may be made for the maintenance and support of the Soldiers' Home in Massachusetts and for free public libraries in any city or town, and to carry out legal obligations, if any, already entered into; and no such grant, appropriation or use of public money or property or loan of public credit shall be made or authorized for the purpose of founding, maintaining or aiding any church, religious denomination or society.]

Section 3. Nothing herein contained shall be construed to prevent the commonwealth, or any political division thereof, from paying to privately controlled hospitals, infirmaries, or institutions for the deaf, dumb or blind not more than the ordinary and reasonable compensation for care or support actually rendered or furnished by such hospitals, infirmaries or institutions to such persons as may be in whole or in part unable to support or care for themselves.

Section 4. Nothing herein contained shall be construed to deprive any inmate of a publicly controlled reformatory, penal or charitable institution of the opportunity of religious exercises therein of his own faith; but no inmate of such institution shall be compelled to attend religious services or receive religious instruction against his will, or, if a minor, without the consent of his parent or guardian.

Section 5. This amendment shall not take effect until the October first next succeeding its ratification and adoption by the people. [See Amendments, Articles XLVIII, The Initiative, Section 2., LXII, XCV, section 1 and CIII]

Article XLVII.

The maintenance and distribution at reasonable rates, during time of war, public exigency, emergency or distress, of a sufficient supply of food and other common necessaries of life and the providing of shelter, are public functions, and the commonwealth and the cities and towns therein may take and may provide the same for their inhabitants in such manner as the general court shall determine.

Article XLVIII.

I. Definition.

Legislative power shall continue to be vested in the general court; but the people reserve to themselves the popular initiative, which is the power of a specified number of voters to submit constitutional amendments and laws to the people for approval or rejection; and the popular referendum, which is the power of a specified number of voters to submit laws, enacted by the general court, to the people for their ratification or rejection.

The Initiative:

II. Initiative Petitions

Section 1. Contents. - An initiative petition shall set forth the full text of the constitutional amendment or law, hereinafter designated as the measure, which is proposed by the petition.

Section 2. Excluded Matters. - No measure that relates to religion, religious practices or religious institutions; or to the appointment, qualification, tenure, removal, recall or compensation of judges; or to the reversal of a judicial decision; or to the powers, creation or abolition of courts; or the operation of which is restricted to a particular town, city or other political division or to particular districts or localities of the commonwealth; or that makes a specific appropriation of money from the treasury of the commonwealth, shall be proposed by an initiative petition; but if a law approved by the people is not repealed, the general court shall raise by taxation or otherwise and shall appropriate such money as may be necessary to carry such law into effect.

Neither the eighteenth amendment of the constitution, as approved and ratified to take effect on the first day of October in the year nineteen hundred and eighteen, nor this provision for its protection, shall be the subject of an initiative amendment.
No proposition inconsistent with any one of the following rights of the individual, as at present declared in the declaration of rights, shall be the subject of an initiative or referendum petition: The right to receive compensation for private property appropriated to public use; the right of access to and protection in courts of justice; the right of trial by jury; protection from unreasonable search, unreasonable bail and the law martial; freedom of the press; freedom of speech; freedom of elections; and the right of peaceable assembly.

No part of the constitution specifically excluding any matter from the operation of the popular initiative and referendum shall be the subject of an initiative petition; nor shall this section be the subject of such a petition.

The limitations on the legislative power of the general court in the constitution shall extend to the legislative power of the people as exercised hereunder.

Section 3. Mode of Originating. - Such petition shall first be signed by ten qualified voters of the commonwealth and shall then be submitted to the attorney-general, and if he shall certify that the measure is in proper form for submission to the people, and that it is not, either affirmatively or negatively, substantially the same as any measure which has been qualified for submission or submitted to the people within three years of the succeeding first Wednesday in December and that it contains only subjects not excluded from the popular initiative and which are related or which are mutually dependent, it may then be filed with the secretary of the commonwealth. The secretary of the commonwealth shall provide blanks for the use of subsequent signers, and shall print at the top of each blank a description of the proposed measure as such description will appear on the ballot together with the names and residences of the first ten signers. All initiative petitions, with the first ten signatures attached, shall be filed with the secretary of the commonwealth not earlier than the first Wednesday of the September before the assembling of the general court into which they are to be introduced, and the remainder of the required signatures shall be filed not later than the first Wednesday of the following December.] [Section 3 superseded by section 1 of Amendments, Article LXXIV]

Section 4. Transmission to the General Court. - If an initiative petition, signed by the required number of qualified voters, has been filed as aforesaid, the secretary of the commonwealth shall, upon the assembling of the general court, transmit it to the clerk of the house of representatives, and the proposed measure shall then be deemed to be introduced and pending.

III. Legislative Action. General Provisions

Section 1. Reference to Committee. - If a measure is introduced into the general court by initiative petition, it shall be referred to a committee thereof, and the petitioners and all parties in interest shall be heard, and the measure shall be considered and reported upon to the general court with the committee's recommendations, and the reasons therefor, in writing. Majority and minority reports shall be signed by the members of said committee.

Section 2. Legislative Substitutes. - The general court may, by resolution passed by yea and nay vote, either by the two houses separately, or in the case of a constitutional amendment by a majority of those voting thereon in joint session in each of two years as hereinafter provided, submit to the people a substitute for any measure introduced by initiative petition, such substitute to be designated on the ballot as the legislative substitute for such an initiative measure and to be grouped with it as an alternative therefor.

IV. Legislative Action on Proposed Constitutional Amendments

Section 1. Definition. - A proposal for amendment to the constitution introduced into the general court by initiative petition shall be designated an initiative amendment, and an amendment introduced by a member of either house shall be designated a legislative substitute or a legislative amendment.

Section 2. Joint Session. - If a proposal for a specific amendment of the constitution is introduced into the general court by initiative petition signed by not less than twenty-five thousand qualified voters, or if in case of a proposal for amendment introduced into the general court by a member of either house, consideration thereof in joint session is called for by vote of either house, such proposal shall, not later than the second Wednesday in June, be laid before a joint session of the two houses, at which the president of the senate shall preside; and if the two houses fail to agree upon a time for holding any joint session hereby required, or fail to continue the same from time to time until final action has been taken upon all amendments pending, the governor shall call such joint session or continuance thereof.] [Section 2 superseded by section 1 of Amendments, Article LXXXI]

Section 3. Amendment of Proposed Amendments. - A proposal for an amendment to the constitution introduced by initiative petition shall be voted upon in the form in which it was introduced, unless such amendment is amended by vote of three-fourths of the members voting thereon in joint session, which vote shall be taken by call of the yeas and nays if called for by any member.

Section 4. Legislative Action. - Final legislative action in the joint session upon any amendment shall be taken only by call of the yeas and nays, which shall be entered upon the journals of the two houses; and an unfavorable vote at any stage preceding final action shall be verified by call of the yeas and nays, to be entered in like manner. At such joint session a legislative amendment receiving the affirmative votes of a majority of all the members elected, or an initiative amendment receiving the affirmative votes of not less than one-fourth of all the members elected, shall be referred to the next general court.

Section 5. Submission to the People. If in the next general court a legislative amendment shall again be agreed to in joint session by a majority of all the members elected, or if an initiative amendment or a legislative substitute shall again receive the affirmative votes of a least one-fourth of all the members elected, such fact shall be certified by the clerk of such joint session to the secretary of the commonwealth, who shall submit the amendment to the people at the next state election. Such amendment shall become part of the constitution if approved, in the case of a legislative amendment, by a majority of the voters voting thereon, or if approved, in the case of an initiative amendment or a legislative substitute, by voters equal in number to at least thirty per cent of the total number of ballots cast at such state election and also by a majority of the voters voting on such amendment.

V. Legislative Action on Proposed Laws.

Section 1. Legislative Procedure. - If an initiative petition for a law is introduced into the general court, signed by not less than twenty thousand qualified voters, a vote shall be taken by yeas and nays in both houses before the first Wednesday of June upon the enactment of such law in the form in which it stands in such petition. If the general court fails to enact such law before the first Wednesday of June, and if such petition is completed by filing with the secretary of the commonwealth, not earlier than the first Wednesday of the following July nor later than the first Wednesday of the following August, not less than five thousand signatures of qualified voters, in addition to those signing such initiative petition, which signatures must have been obtained after the first Wednesday of June aforesaid, then the secretary of the commonwealth shall submit such proposed law to the people at the next state election. If it shall be approved by voters equal in number to at least thirty per cent of the total number of ballots cast at such state election and also by a majority of the voters voting on such law, it shall become law, and shall take effect in thirty days after such state election or at such time after such election as may be provided in such law.] [Section 1 superseded by section 2 of Amendments, Article LXXXI]

Section 2. Amendment by Petitioners. - If the general court fails to pass a proposed law before the first Wednesday of June, a majority of the first ten signers of the initiative petition therefor shall have the right, subject to certification by the attorney-general filed as hereinafter provided, to amend the measure which is the subject of such petition. An amendment so made shall not invalidate any signature attached to the petition. If the measure so amended, signed by a majority of the first ten signers, is filed with the secretary of the commonwealth before the first Wednesday of the following July, together with a certificate signed by the attorney-general to the effect that the amendment made by such proposers is in his opinion perfecting in its nature and does not materially change the substance of the measure, and if such petition is completed by filing with the secretary of the commonwealth, not earlier than the first Wednesday of the following July nor later than the first Wednesday of the following August, not less than five thousand signatures of qualified voters, in addition to those signing such initiative petition, which signatures must have been obtained after the first Wednesday of June aforesaid, then the secretary of the commonwealth shall submit the measure to the people in its amended form.] [Section 2 superseded by section 3 of Amendments, Article LXXXI]

VI. Conflicting and Alternative Measures.

If in any judicial proceeding, provisions of constitutional amendments or of laws approved by the people at the same election are held to be in conflict, then the provisions contained in the measure that received the largest number of affirmative votes at such election shall govern.

A constitutional amendment approved at any election shall govern any law approved at the same election.

The general court, by resolution passed as hereinbefore set forth, may provide for grouping and designating upon the ballot as conflicting measures or as alternative measures, only one of which is to be adopted, any two or more proposed constitutional amendments or laws which have been or may be passed or qualified for submission to the people at any one election: provided, that a proposed constitutional amendment and a proposed law shall not be so grouped, and that the ballot shall afford an opportunity to the voter to vote for each of the measures or for only one of the measures, as may be provided in said resolution, or against each of the measures so grouped as conflicting or as alternative. In case more than one of the measures so grouped shall receive the vote required for its approval as herein provided, only that one for which the largest affirmative vote was cast shall be deemed to be approved.
The Referendum.

I. When Statutes shall take Effect.

No law passed by the general court shall take effect earlier than ninety days after it has become a law, excepting laws declared to be emergency laws and laws which may not be made the subject of a referendum petition, as herein provided.

II. Emergency Measures.

A law declared to be an emergency law shall contain a preamble setting forth the facts constituting the emergency, and shall contain the statement that such law is necessary for the immediate preservation of the public peace, health, safety or convenience. [A separate vote shall be taken on the preamble by call of the yeas and nays, which shall be recorded, and unless the preamble is adopted by two-thirds of the members of each house voting thereon, the law shall not be an emergency law; but] if the governor, at any time before the election at which it is to be submitted to the people on referendum, files with the secretary of the commonwealth a statement declaring that in his opinion the immediate preservation of the public peace, health, safety or convenience requires that such law should take effect forthwith and that it is an emergency law and setting forth the facts constituting the emergency, then such law, if not previously suspended as hereinafter provided, shall take effect without suspension, or if such law has been so suspended such suspension shall thereupon terminate and such law shall thereupon take effect: but no grant of any franchise or amendment thereof, or renewal or extension thereof for more than one year shall be declared to be an emergency law. [See Amendments, Article [See Amendments, Article LXVII.]

III. Referendum Petitions.

Section 1. Contents. - A referendum petition may ask for a referendum to the people upon any law enacted by the general court which is not herein expressly excluded.

Section 2. Excluded Matters. - No law that relates to religion, religious practices or religious institutions; or to the appointment, qualification, tenure, removal or compensation of judges; or to the powers, creation or abolition of courts; or the operation of which is restricted to a particular town, city or other political division or to particular districts or localities of the commonwealth; or that appropriates money for the current or ordinary expenses of the commonwealth or for any of its departments, boards, commissions or institutions shall be the subject of a referendum petition.

Section 3. Mode of Petitioning for the Suspension of a Law and a Referendum Thereon. - A petition asking for a referendum on a law, and requesting that the operation of such law be suspended, shall first be signed by ten qualified voters and shall then be filed with the secretary of the commonwealth not later than thirty days after the law that is the subject of the petition has become law. [The secretary of the commonwealth shall provide blanks for the use of subsequent signers, and shall print at the top of each blank a description of the proposed law as such description will appear on the ballot together with the names and residences of the first ten signers. If such petition is completed by filing with the secretary of the commonwealth not later than ninety days after the law which is the subject of the petition has become law the signatures of not less than fifteen thousand qualified voters of the commonwealth, then the operation of such law shall be suspended, and the secretary of the commonwealth shall submit such law to the people at the next state election, if thirty days intervene between the date when such petition is filed with the secretary of the commonwealth and the date for holding such state election; if thirty days do not so intervene, then such law shall be submitted to the people at the next following state election, unless in the meantime it shall have been repealed; and if it shall be approved by a majority of the qualified voters voting thereon, such law shall, subject to the provisions of the constitution, take effect in thirty days after such election, or at such time after such election as may be provided in such law; if not so approved such law shall be null and void; but no such law shall be held to be disapproved if the negative vote is less than thirty per cent of the total number of ballots cast at such state election.] [Section 3 amended by section 2 of Amendments, Article LXXIV and section 4 of Amendments, Article LXXXI]

Section 4. Petitions for Referendum on an Emergency Law or a Law the Suspension of Which is Not Asked for. - A referendum petition may ask for the repeal of an emergency law or of a law which takes effect because the referendum petition does not contain a request for suspension, as aforesaid. Such petition shall first be signed by ten qualified voters of the commonwealth, and shall then be filed with the secretary of the commonwealth not later than thirty days after the law which is the subject of the petition has become law. [The secretary of the commonwealth shall provide blanks for the use of subsequent signers, and shall print at the top of each blank a description of the proposed law as such description will appear on the ballot together with the names and residences of the first ten signers. If such petition filed as aforesaid is completed by filing with the secretary of the commonwealth not later than ninety days after the law which is the subject of the petition has become law the signatures of not less than ten thousand qualified voters of the commonwealth protesting against such law and asking for a referendum thereon, then the secretary of the commonwealth shall submit such law to the people at the next state election, if thirty days intervene between the date when such petition is filed with the secretary of the commonwealth and the date for holding such state election. If thirty days do not so intervene, then it shall be submitted to the people at the next following state election, unless in the meantime it shall have been repealed; and if it shall not be approved by a majority of the qualified voters voting thereon, it shall, at the expiration of thirty days after such election, be thereby repealed; but no such law shall be held to be disapproved if the negative vote is less than thirty per cent of the total number of ballots cast at such state election.] [Section 4 superseded by section 3 of Amendments, Article LXXIV and section 5 of Amendments, Article LXXXI]

General Provisions.

I. Identification and Certification of Signatures.

Provision shall be made by law for the proper identification and certification of signatures to the petitions hereinbefore referred to, and for penalties for signing any such petition, or refusing to sign it, for money or other valuable consideration, and for the forgery of signatures thereto. Pending the passage of such legislation all provisions of law relating to the identification and certification of signatures to petitions for the nomination of candidates for state offices or to penalties for the forgery of such signatures shall apply to the signatures to the petitions herein referred to. The general court may provide by law that no co-partnership or corporation shall undertake for hire or reward to circulate petitions, may require individuals who circulate petitions for hire or reward to be licensed, and may make other reasonable regulations to prevent abuses arising from the circulation of petitions for hire or reward.

II. Limitation on Signatures.

Not more than one-fourth of the certified signatures on any petition shall be those of registered voters of any one county.

III. Form of Ballot.

Each proposed amendment to the constitution, and each law submitted to the people, shall be described on the ballots by a description to be determined by the attorney-general, subject to such provision as may be made by law, and the secretary of the commonwealth shall give each question a number and cause such question, except as otherwise authorized herein, to be printed on the ballot in the following form:-

In the case of an amendment to the constitution: Shall an amendment to the constitution (here insert description, and state, in distinctive type, whether approved or disapproved by the general court, and by what vote thereon) be approved?
In the case of a law: Shall a law (here insert description, and state, in distinctive type, whether approved or disapproved by the general court, and by what vote thereon) be approved?

IV. Information for Voters.

The secretary of the commonwealth shall cause to be printed and sent to each registered voter in the commonwealth the full text of every measure to be submitted to the people, together with a copy of the legislative committee's majority and minority reports, if there be such, with the names of the majority and minority members thereon, a statement of the votes of the general court on the measure, and a description of the measure as such description will appear on the ballot; and shall, in such manner as may be provided by law, cause to be prepared and sent to the voters other information and arguments for and against the measure.] [Subheadings III and IV superseded by section 4 of Amendments, Article LXXIV][Subheading IV superseded by Amendments, Article CVIII]

V. The Veto Power of the Governor.

Subject to the veto power of the governor and to the right of referendum by petition as herein provided, the general court may amend or repeal a law approved by the people.

VI. The General Court's Power of Repeal.

Subject to the veto power of the governor and to the right of referendum by petition as herein provided, the general court may amend or repeal a law approved by the people.

VII. Amendment Declared to be Self-executing.

This article of amendment to the constitution is self-executing, but legislation not inconsistent with anything herein contained may be enacted to facilitate the operation of its provisions.

VIII. Articles IX and XLII of Amendments of the Constitution Annulled.

Article IX and Article XLII of the amendments of the constitution are hereby annulled.

Article XLIX.

[The conservation, development and utilization of the agricultural, mineral, forest, water and other natural resources of the commonwealth are public uses, and the general court shall have power to provide for the taking, upon payment of just compensation therefor, of lands and easements or interests therein, including water and mineral rights, for the purpose of securing and promoting the proper conservation, development, utilization and control thereof and to enact legislation necessary or expedient therefor.] [Superseded by Amendments, Article XCVII]

Article L.

Advertising on public ways, in public places and on private property within public view may be regulated and restricted by law.

Article LI.

The preservation and maintenance of ancient landmarks and other property of historical or antiquarian interest is a public use, and the commonwealth and the cities and towns therein may, upon payment of just compensation, take such property or any interest therein under such regulations as the general court may prescribe.

Article LII.

[The general court, by concurrent vote of the two houses, may take a recess or recesses amounting to not more than thirty days; but no such recess shall extend beyond the sixtieth day from the date of their first assembling.] [Superseded by Amendments, Article CII]

Article LIII.

Article X of Section I of Chapter II of the constitution, the last two paragraphs of Article IV of the articles of amendment, relating to the appointment of a commissary general and the removal of militia officers, and Article V of the articles of amendment are hereby annulled, and the following is adopted in place thereof:

Article X – All military and naval officers shall be selected and appointed and may be removed in such manner as the general court may by law prescribe, but no such officer shall be appointed unless he shall have passed an examination prepared by a competent commission or shall have served one year in either the federal or state militia or in military service. All such officers who are entitled by law to receive commissions shall be commissioned by the governor.

Article LIV.

Article VII of Section I of Chapter II of the constitution is hereby annulled and the following is adopted in place thereof:

Article VII. The general court shall provide by law for the recruitment, equipment, organization, training and discipline of the military and naval forces. The governor shall be the commander-in-chief thereof, and shall have power to assemble the whole or any part of them for training, instruction or parade, and to employ them for the suppression of rebellion, the repelling of invasion, and the enforcement of the laws. He may, as authorized by the general court, prescribe from time to time the organization of the military and naval forces and make regulations for their government.

Article LV.

Article VI of Section III of Chapter II of the constitution is hereby annulled and the following is adopted in place thereof:

Whenever the offices of governor and lieutenant-governor shall both be vacant, by reason of death, absence from the commonwealth, or otherwise, then one of the following officers, in the order of succession herein named, namely, the secretary, attorney-general, treasurer and receiver-general, and auditor, shall, during such vacancy, have full power and authority to do and execute all and every such acts, matters and things as the governor or the lieutenant-governor might or could lawfully do or execute, if they, or either of them, were personally present.

Article LVI.

[The governor, within five days after any bill or resolve shall have been laid before him, shall have the right to return it to the branch of the general court in which it originated with a recommendation that any amendment or amendments specified by him be made therein. Such bill or resolve shall thereupon be before the general court and subject to amendment and re-enactment. If such bill or resolve is re-enacted in any form it shall again be laid before the governor for his action, but he shall have no right to return the same a second time with a recommendation to amend.] [Superseded by Amendments, Article XC, Section 3]

Article LVII.

Article IV of the articles of amendment of the constitution of the commonwealth is hereby amended by adding thereto the following words: -- Women shall be eligible to appointment as notaries public. [Change of name shall render the commission void, but shall not prevent reappointment under the new name.] [See Amendments, Article LXIX]

Article LVIII.

Article I of Chapter III of Part the Second of the constitution is hereby amended by the addition of the following words: -- and provided also that the governor, with the consent of the council, may after due notice and hearing retire them because of advanced age or mental or physical disability. Such retirement shall be subject to any provisions made by law as to pensions or allowances payable to such officers upon their voluntary retirement. [Superseded by Amendments, Article XCVIII]

Article LIX.

Every charter, franchise or act of incorporation shall forever remain subject to revocation and amendment

Article LX.

The general court shall have power to limit buildings according to their use or construction to specified districts of cities and towns.

Article LXI.

The general court shall have authority to provide for compulsory voting at elections, but the right of secret voting shall be preserved.

Article LXII.

Section 1. The credit of the commonwealth shall not in any manner be given or loaned to or in aid of any individual, or of any private association, or of any corporation which is privately owned and managed.] [Superseded by Amendments, Article LXXXIV]

Section 2. The commonwealth may borrow money to repel invasion, suppress insurrection, defend the commonwealth, or to assist the United States in case of war, and may also borrow money in anticipation of receipts from taxes or other sources, such loan to be paid out of the revenue of the year in which it is created.

Section 3. In addition to the loans which may be contracted as before provided, the commonwealth may borrow money only by a vote, taken by the yeas and nays, of two-thirds of each house of the general court present and voting thereon. The governor shall recommend to the general court the term for which any loan shall be contracted.

Section 4. Borrowed money shall not be expended for any other purpose than that for which it was borrowed or for the reduction or discharge of the principal of the loan.

Article LXIII.

Section 1. Collection of Revenue. - All money received on account of the commonwealth from any source whatsoever shall be paid into the treasury thereof.

Section 2. The Budget. - Within three weeks after the convening of the general court the governor shall recommend to the general court a budget which shall contain a statement of all proposed expenditures of the commonwealth for the fiscal year, including those already authorized by law, and of all taxes, revenues, loans and other means by which such expenditures shall be defrayed. This shall be arranged in such form as the general court may by law prescribe, or, in default thereof, as the governor shall determine. For the purpose of preparing his budget, the governor shall have power to require any board, commission, officer, or department to furnish him with any information which he may deem necessary.] [See Amendments, Articles LXXII and LXXV] [Annulled by Amendments, Article CVII]

Section 3. The General Appropriation Bill. - All appropriations based upon the budget to be paid from taxes or revenues shall be incorporated in a single bill which shall be called the general appropriation bill. The general court may increase, decrease, add or omit items in the budget. The general court may provide for its salaries, mileage, and expenses and for necessary expenditures in anticipation of appropriations, but before final action on the general appropriation bill it shall not enact any other appropriation bill except on recommendation of the governor. The governor may at any time recommend to the general court supplementary budgets which shall be subject to the same procedures as the original budget.

Section 4. Special Appropriation Bills. - After final action on the general appropriation bill or on recommendation of the governor, special appropriation bills may be enacted. Such bills shall provide the specific means for defraying the appropriations therein contained.

Section 5. Submission to the Governor. - The governor may disapprove or reduce items or parts of items in any bill appropriating money. So much of such bill as he approves shall upon his signing the same become law. As to each item disapproved or reduced, he shall transmit to the house in which the bill originated his reason for such disapproval or reduction, and the procedure shall then be the same as in the case of a bill disapproved as a whole. In case he shall fail so to transmit his reasons for such disapproval or reduction within five days after the bill shall have been presented to him, such items shall have the force of law unless the general court by adjournment shall prevent such transmission, in which case they shall not be law.] [See Amendments, Article XC, Section 4]

Article LXIV.

Section 1. The governor, lieutenant-governor, councillors, secretary, treasurer and receiver-general, attorney-general, auditor, senators and representatives, shall be elected biennially. The governor, lieutenant-governor and councillors shall hold their respective offices from the first Wednesday in January succeeding their election to and including the first Wednesday in January in the third year following their election and until their successors are chosen and qualified. The terms of senators and representatives shall begin with the first Wednesday in January succeeding their election and shall extend to the first Wednesday in January in the third year following their election and until their successors are chosen and qualified. The terms of the secretary, treasurer and receiver-general, attorney-general and auditor, shall begin with the third Wednesday in January succeeding their election and shall extend to the third Wednesday in January in the third year following their election and until their successors are chosen and qualified.] [Superseded by Amendments, Article LXXX]

Section 2. No person shall be eligible to election to the office of treasurer and receiver-general for more than three successive terms. [Annulled by Amendments, Article LXXXII]

Section 3. The general court shall assemble every year on the first Wednesday in January. [See Amendments, Articles LXXII and LXXV]

Section 4. The first election to which this article shall apply shall be held on the Tuesday next after the first Monday in November in the year nineteen hundred and twenty, and thereafter elections for the choice of all the officers before-mentioned shall be held biennially on the Tuesday next after the first Monday in November.] [Annulled and superseded by Amendments, Article LXXXII]

Article LXV.

No person elected to the general court shall during the term for which he was elected be appointed to any office created or the emoluments whereof are increased during such term, nor receive additional salary or compensation for service upon any recess committee or commission except a committee appointed to examine a general revision of the statutes of the commonwealth when submitted to the general court for adoption.

Article LXVI.

On or before January first, nineteen hundred twenty-one, the executive and administrative work of the commonwealth shall be organized in not more than twenty departments, in one of which every executive and administrative office, board and commission, except those officers serving directly under the governor or the council, shall be placed. Such departments shall be under such supervision and regulation as the general court may from time to time prescribe by law. [Annulled by Amendments, Article LXXXVII]

Article LXVII.

Article XLVIII of the Amendments to the Constitution is hereby amended by striking out, in that part entitled "II. Emergency Measures", under the heading "The Referendum", the words "A separate vote shall be taken on the preamble by call of the yeas and nays, which shall be recorded, and unless the preamble is adopted by two-thirds of the members of each House voting thereon, the law shall not be an emergency law; but" and substituting the following: -- A separate vote, which shall be recorded, shall be taken on the preamble, and unless the preamble is adopted by two-thirds of the members of each House voting thereon, the law shall not be an emergency law. Upon the request of two members of the Senate or of five members of the House of Representatives, the vote on the preamble in such branch shall be taken by call of the yeas and nays. But

Article LXVIII.

Article III of the amendments to the constitution, as amended, is hereby further amended by striking out, in the first line, the word "male".

Article LXIX.

Section 1. No person shall be deemed to be ineligible to hold state, county or municipal office by reason of sex.

Section 2. Article IV of the articles of amendment of the constitution of the commonwealth, as amended by Article LVII of said amendments, is hereby further amended by striking out the words "Change of name shall render the commission void, but shall not prevent reappointment under the new name", and inserting in place thereof the following words: -- Upon the change of name of any woman, she shall re-register under her new name and shall pay such fee therefor as shall be established by the general court.

Article LXX.

Article II of the articles of amendment to the constitution of the commonwealth is hereby amended by adding at the end thereof the following new paragraph: --

Nothing in this article shall prevent the general court from establishing in any corporate town or towns in this commonwealth containing more than six thousand inhabitants a form of town government providing for a town meeting limited to such inhabitants of the town as may be elected to meet, deliberate, act and vote in the exercise of the corporate powers of the town subject to such restrictions and regulations as the general court may prescribe; provided, that such establishment be with the consent, and on the application of a majority of the inhabitants of such town, present and voting thereon, pursuant to a vote at a meeting duly warned and holden for that purpose. [Annulled by Amendments, Article LXXXIX]

Article LXXI.

[Article XXI of the articles of amendment is hereby annulled and the following is adopted in place thereof:

Article XXI. – In the year nineteen hundred and thirty-five and every tenth year thereafter a census of the inhabitants of each city and town shall be taken and a special enumeration shall be made of the legal voters therein. Said special enumeration shall also specify the number of legal voters residing in each precinct of each town containing twelve thousand or more inhabitants according to said census and in each ward of each city. Each special enumeration shall be the basis for determining the representative districts for the ten year period beginning with the first Wednesday in the fourth January following said special enumeration; provided, that such districts as established in the year nineteen hundred and twenty-six shall continue in effect until the first Wednesday in January in the year nineteen hundred and thirty-nine.

The house of representatives shall consist of two hundred and forty members, which shall be apportioned by the general court, at its first regular session after the return of each special enumeration, to the several counties of the commonwealth, equally, as nearly as may be, according to their relative numbers of legal voters, as ascertained by said special enumeration; and the town of Cohasset, in the county of Norfolk, shall, for this purpose, as well as in the formation of districts as hereinafter provided, be considered a part of the county of Plymouth; and it shall be the duty of the secretary of the commonwealth to certify, as soon as may be after it is determined by the general court, the number of representatives to which each county shall be entitled, to the board authorized to divide such county into representative districts. The county commissioners or other body acting as such or, in lieu thereof, such board of special commissioners in each county as may for that purpose be provided by law, shall, within thirty days after such certification by the secretary of the commonwealth or within such other period as the general court may by law provide, assemble at a shire town of their respective counties, and proceed, as soon as may be, to divide the same into representative districts of contiguous territory and assign representatives thereto, so that each representative in such county will represent an equal number of legal voters, as nearly as may be; and such districts shall be so formed that no town containing less than twelve thousand inhabitants according to said census, no precinct of any other town and no ward of a city shall be divided therefor, nor shall any district be made which shall be entitled to elect more than three representatives. The general court may by law limit the time within which judicial proceedings may be instituted calling in question any such apportionment, division or assignment. Every representative, for one year at least immediately preceding his election, shall have been an inhabitant of the district for which he is chosen and shall cease to represent such district when he shall cease to be an inhabitant of the commonwealth. The districts in each county shall be numbered by the board creating the same, and a description of each, with the numbers thereof and the number of legal voters therein, shall be returned by the board, to the secretary of the commonwealth, the county treasurer of such county, and to the clerk of every city or town in such county, to be filed and kept in their respective offices. The manner of calling and conducting the elections for the choice of representatives, and of ascertaining their election, shall be prescribed by law.

Article XXII of the articles of amendment is hereby annulled and the following is adopted in place thereof:

Article XXII. Each special enumeration of legal voters required in the preceding article of amendment shall likewise be the basis for determining the senatorial districts and also the councillor districts for the ten year period beginning with the first Wednesday in the fourth January following such enumeration; provided, that such districts as established in the year nineteen hundred and twenty-six shall continue in effect until the first Wednesday in January in the year nineteen hundred and thirty-nine. The senate shall consist of forty members. The general court shall, at its first regular session after the return of each special enumeration, divide the commonwealth into forty districts of contiguous territory, each district to contain, as nearly as may be, an equal number of legal voters, according to said special enumeration; provided, however, that no town or ward of a city shall be divided therefor; and such districts shall be formed, as nearly as may be, without uniting two counties, or parts of two or more counties, into one district. The general court may by law limit the time within which judicial proceedings may be instituted calling in question such division. Each district shall elect one senator, who shall have been an inhabitant of this commonwealth five years at least immediately preceding his election, and at the time of his election shall be an inhabitant of the district for which he is chosen; and he shall cease to represent such senatorial district when he shall cease to be an inhabitant of the commonwealth. [Superseded by Amendments, Articles XCII, CI and CIX]

Article LXXII.

[**Section 1.** The general court shall assemble in regular session on the first Wednesday of January in the year following the approval of this article and biennially on said Wednesday thereafter. Nothing herein contained shall prevent the general court from assembling at such other times as they shall judge necessary or when called together by the governor."

Section 2. The budget required by Section 2 of Article LXIII of the amendments to the constitution shall be for the year in which the same is adopted and for the ensuing year."
Section 3. All provisions of this constitution and of the amendments thereto requiring the general court to meet annually are hereby annulled."] [Annulled by Amendments, Article LXXV]

Article LXXIII.

Article VIII of section I of chapter II of Part the Second of the Constitution of the Commonwealth is hereby annulled and the following is adopted in place thereof:--

Article VIII. The power of pardoning offences, except such as persons may be convicted of before the senate by an impeachment of the house, shall be in the governor, by and with the advice of council, provided, that if the offence is a felony the general court shall have power to prescribe the terms and conditions upon which a pardon may be granted; but no charter of pardon, granted by the governor, with advice of the council before conviction, shall avail the party pleading the same, notwithstanding any general or particular expressions contained therein, descriptive of the offence or offences intended to be pardoned.

Article LXXIV.

Section 1. Article XLVIII of the amendments to the constitution is hereby amended by striking out section three, under the heading "THE INITIATIVE. III. Initiative Petitions.", and inserting in place thereof the following: -

Section 3. Mode of Originating. - Such petition shall first be signed by ten qualified voters of the commonwealth and shall be submitted to the attorney-general not later than the first Wednesday of the August before the assembling of the general court into which it is to be introduced, and if he shall certify that the measure and the title thereof are in proper form for submission to the people, and that the measure is not, either affirmatively or negatively, substantially the same as any measure which has been qualified for submission or submitted to the people at either of the two preceding biennial state elections, and that it contains only subjects not excluded from the popular initiative and which are related or which are mutually dependent, it may then be filed with the secretary of the commonwealth. The secretary of the commonwealth shall provide blanks for the use of subsequent signers, and shall print at the top of each blank a fair, concise summary, as determined by the attorney-general, of the proposed measure as such summary will appear on the ballot together with the names and residences of the first ten signers. All initiative petitions, with the first ten signatures attached, shall be filed with the secretary of the commonwealth not earlier than the first Wednesday of the September before the assembling of the general court into which they are to be introduced, and the remainder of the required signatures shall be filed not later than the first Wednesday of the following December.

Section 2. Section three of that part of said Article XLVIII, under the heading "THE REFERENDUM. III. Referendum Petitions.", is hereby amended by striking out the words "The secretary of the commonwealth shall provide blanks for the use of subsequent signers, and shall print at the top of each blank a description of the proposed law as such description will appear on the ballot together with the names and residences of the first ten signers.", and inserting in place thereof the words "The secretary of the commonwealth shall provide blanks for the use of subsequent signers, and shall print at the top of each blank a fair, concise summary of the proposed law as such summary will appear on the ballot together with the names and residences of the first ten signers."

Section 3. Section four of that part of said Article XLVIII under the heading "THE REFERENDUM. III. Referendum Petitions.", is hereby amended by striking out the words "The secretary of the commonwealth shall provide blanks for the use of subsequent signers, and shall print at the top of each blank a description of the proposed law as such description will appear on the ballot together with the names and residences of the first ten signers.", and inserting in place thereof the words "The secretary of the commonwealth shall provide blanks for the use of subsequent signers, and shall print at the top of each blank a fair, concise summary of the proposed law as such summary will appear on the ballot together with the names and residences of the first ten signers."

Section 4. Said Article XLVIII is hereby further amended by striking out, under the heading "GENERAL PROVISIONS", all of subheading "III. Form of Ballot." and all of subheading "IV. Information for Voters.", and inserting in place thereof the following:--

III. Form of Ballot.

A fair, concise summary, as determined by the attorney general, subject to such provision as may be made by law, of each proposed amendment to the constitution, and each law submitted to the people, shall be printed on the ballot, and the secretary of the commonwealth shall give each question a number and cause such question, except as otherwise authorized herein, to be printed on the ballot in the following form:--

In the case of an amendment to the constitution: Do you approve of the adoption of an amendment to the constitution summarized below, (here state, in distinctive type, whether approved or disapproved by the general court, and by what vote thereon)?

[Set forth summary here]

In the case of a law: Do you approve of a law summarized below, (here state, in distinctive type, whether approved or disapproved by the general court, and by what vote thereon)?
[Set forth summary here]

IV. Information for Voters.

The secretary of the commonwealth shall cause to be printed and sent to each registered voter in the commonwealth the full text of every measure to be submitted to the people, together with a copy of the legislative committee's majority and minority reports, if there be such, with the names of the majority and minority members thereon, a statement of the votes of the general court on the measure, and a fair, concise summary of the measure as such summary will appear on the ballot; and shall, in such manner as may be provided by law, cause to be prepared and sent to the voters other information and arguments for and against the measure.] [See Amendments, Article CVIII]

Article LXXV.

Article LXXII of the amendments to the constitution providing for biennial sessions of the general court and a biennial budget is hereby annulled, and all provisions of this constitution and of the amendments thereto which were annulled or affected by said Article shall have the same force and effect as though said Article had not been adopted.

Article LXXVI.

Article XLV of the articles of amendment is hereby annulled and the following is adopted in place thereof:--
Article XLV. The general court shall have power to provide by law for voting, in the choice of any officer to be elected or upon any question submitted at an election, by qualified voters of the commonwealth who, at the time of such an election, are absent from the city or town of which they are inhabitants or are unable by reason of physical disability to cast their votes in person at the polling places. [Superseded by Amendments, Article CV]

Article LXXVII.

Article XVI of Part the First is hereby annulled and the following is adopted in place thereof:

Article XVI. The liberty of the press is essential to the security of freedom in a state: it ought not, therefore, to be restrained in this commonwealth. The right of free speech shall not be abridged.

Article LXXVIII.

No revenue from fees, duties, excises or license taxes relating to registration, operation or use of vehicles on public highways, or to fuels used for propelling such vehicles, shall be expended for other than cost of administration of laws providing for such revenue, making of refunds and adjustments in relation thereto, payment of highway obligations, or cost of construction, reconstruction, maintenance and repair of public highways and bridges and of the enforcement of state traffic laws; and such revenue shall be expended by the commonwealth or its counties, cities and towns for said highway purposes only and in such manner as the general court may direct; provided, that this amendment shall not apply to revenue from any excise tax imposed in lieu of local property taxes for the privilege of registering such vehicles. [Annulled by Amendments, Article CIV]

Article LXXIX.

Article XVII of the amendments of the constitution, as amended, is hereby further amended by striking out, in the third sentence, the words "two persons who had the highest number of votes for said offices on the day in November aforesaid" and inserting in place thereof the words: - people at large, - so that said sentence will read as follows: - In case of a failure to elect either of said officers on the day in November aforesaid, or in case of the decease, in the meantime, of the person elected as such, such officer shall be chosen on or before the third Wednesday in January next thereafter, from the people at large, by joint ballot of the senators and representatives, in one room; and in case the office of secretary, or treasurer and receiver-general, or auditor, or attorney-general, shall become vacant, from any cause, during an annual or special session of the general court, such vacancy shall in like manner be filled by choice from the people at large; but if such vacancy shall occur at any other time, it shall be supplied by the governor by appointment, with the advice and consent of the council.

Article LXXX.

[Article LXIV of the Amendments to the Constitution is hereby amended by striking out section 1 and inserting in place thereof the following section:-

Section 1. The governor, lieutenant-governor, councillors, secretary, treasurer and receiver-general, attorney-general, auditor, senators and representatives shall be elected biennially. The terms of the governor, lieutenant-governor and councillors shall begin at noon on the Thursday next following the first Wednesday in January succeeding their election and shall end at noon on the Thursday next following the first Wednesday in January in the third year following their election. If the governor elect shall have died before the qualification of the lieutenant-governor elect, the lieutenant-governor elect upon qualification shall become governor. If both the governor elect and the lieutenant-governor elect shall have died both said offices shall be deemed to be vacant and the provisions of Article LV of the Amendments to the Constitution shall apply. The terms of senators and representatives shall begin with the first Wednesday in January succeeding their election and shall extend to the first Wednesday in January in the third year following their election and until their successors are chosen and qualified. The terms of the secretary, treasurer and receiver-general, attorney-general and auditor, shall begin with the third Wednesday in January succeeding their election and shall extend to the third Wednesday in January in the third year following their election and until their successors are chosen and qualified.] [Annulled and superseded by Amendments, Article LXXXII.]
Article LXXXI.

Section 1. Article XLVIII of the Amendments to the Constitution is hereby amended by striking out section 2, under the heading

"THE INITIATIVE. IV. Legislative Action on Proposed Constitutional Amendments.", and inserting in place thereof the following:-

Section 2. Joint Session. - If a proposal for a specific amendment of the constitution is introduced into the general court by initiative petition signed in the aggregate by not less than such number of voters as will equal three per cent of the entire vote cast for governor at the preceding biennial state election, or if in case of a proposal for amendment introduced into the general court by a member of either house, consideration thereof in joint session is called for by vote of either house, such proposal shall, not later than the second Wednesday in May, be laid before a joint session of the two houses, at which the president of the senate shall preside; and if the two houses fail to agree upon a time for holding any joint session hereby required, or fail to continue the same from time to time until final action has been taken upon all amendments pending, the governor shall call such joint session or continuance thereof.

Section 2. Section 1 of that part of said Article XLVIII, under the heading "THE INITIATIVE. V. Legislative Action on Proposed Laws.", is hereby amended by striking out said section and inserting in place thereof the following:-

Section 1. Legislative Procedure. - If an initiative petition for a law is introduced into the general court, signed in the aggregate by not less than such number of voters as will equal three per cent of the entire vote cast for governor at the preceding biennial state election, a vote shall be taken by yeas and nays in both houses before the first Wednesday of May upon the enactment of such law in the form in which it stands in such petition. If the general court fails to enact such law before the first Wednesday of May, and if such petition is completed by filing with the secretary of the commonwealth, not earlier than the first Wednesday of the following June nor later than the first Wednesday of the following July, a number of signatures of qualified voters equal in number to not less than one half of one per cent of the entire vote cast for governor at the preceding biennial state election, in addition to those signing such initiative petition, which signatures must have been obtained after the first Wednesday of May aforesaid, then the secretary of the commonwealth shall submit such proposed law to the people at the next state election. If it shall be approved by voters equal in number to at least thirty per cent of the total number of ballots cast at such state election and also by a majority of the voters voting on such law, it shall become law, and shall take effect in thirty days after such state election or at such time after such election as may be provided in such law.

Section 3. Section 2 of that part of said Article XLVIII, under the heading "THE INITIATIVE. V. Legislative Action on Proposed Laws.", is hereby amended by striking out said section and inserting in place thereof the following:-

Section 2. Amendment by Petitioners. If the general court fails to pass a proposed law before the first Wednesday of May, a majority of the first ten signers of the initiative petition therefor shall have the right, subject to certification by the attorney-general filed as hereinafter provided , to amend the measure which is the subject of such petition. An amendment so made shall not invalidate any signature attached to the petition. If the measure so amended, signed by a majority of the first ten signers, is filed with the secretary of the commonwealth before the first Wednesday of the following June, together with a certificate signed by the attorney-general to the effect that the amendment made by such proposers is in his opinion perfecting in its nature and does not materially change the substance of the measure, and if such petition is completed by filing with the secretary of the commonwealth, not earlier than the first Wednesday of the following June nor later than the first Wednesday of the following July, a number of signatures of qualified voters equal in number to not less than one half of one per cent of the entire vote cast for governor at the preceding biennial state election in addition to those signing such initiative petition, which signatures must have been obtained after the first Wednesday of May aforesaid, then the secretary of the commonwealth shall submit the measure to the people in its amended form.

Section 4. Section 3 of that part of said Article XLVIII, under the heading "THE REFERENDUM. III. Referendum Petitions.", is hereby amended by striking out the sentence "If such petition is completed by filing with the secretary of the commonwealth not later than ninety days after the law which is the subject of the petition has become law the signatures of not less than fifteen thousand qualified voters of the commonwealth, then the operation of such law shall be suspended, and the secretary of the commonwealth shall submit such law to the people at the next state election, if thirty days intervene between the date when such petition is filed with the secretary of the commonwealth and the date for holding such state election; if thirty days do not so intervene, then such law shall be submitted to the people at the next following state election, unless in the meantime it shall have been repealed; and if it shall be approved by a majority of the qualified voters voting thereon, such law shall, subject to the provisions of the constitution, take effect in thirty days after such election, or at such time after such election as may be provided in such law; if not so approved such law shall be null and void; but no such law shall be held to be disapproved if the negative vote is less than thirty per cent of the total number of ballots cast at such state election." and inserting in place thereof the following sentence:-- If such petition is completed by filing with the secretary of the commonwealth not later than ninety days after the law which is the subject of the petition has become law a number of signatures of qualified voters equal in number to not less than two per cent of the entire vote cast for governor at the preceding biennial state election, then the operation of such law shall be suspended, and the secretary of the commonwealth shall submit such law to the people at the next state election, if sixty days intervene between the date when such petition is filed with the secretary of the commonwealth and the date for holding such state election; if sixty days do not so intervene, then such law shall be submitted to the people at the next following state election, unless in the meantime it shall have been repealed; and if it shall be approved by a majority of the qualified voters voting thereon, such law shall, subject to the provisions of the constitution, take effect in thirty days after such election, or at such time after such election as may be provided in such law; if not so approved such law shall be null and void; but no such law shall be held to be disapproved if the negative vote is less than thirty per cent of the total number of ballots cast at such state election.

Section 5. Section 4 of that part of said Article XLVIII, under the heading "THE REFERENDUM. III. Referendum Petitions. is hereby amended by striking out the words "If such petition filed as aforesaid is completed by filing with the secretary of the commonwealth not later than ninety days after the law which is the subject of the petition has become law the signatures of not less than ten thousand qualified voters of the commonwealth protesting against such law and asking for a referendum thereon, then the secretary of the commonwealth shall submit such law to the people at the next state election, if thirty days intervene between the date when such petition is filed with the secretary of the commonwealth and the date for holding such state election. If thirty days do not so intervene, then it shall be submitted to the people at the next following state election, unless in the meantime it shall have been repealed; and if it shall not be approved by a majority of the qualified voters voting thereon, it shall, at the expiration of thirty days after such election, be thereby repealed; but no such law shall be held to be disapproved if the negative vote is less than thirty per cent of the total number of ballots cast at such state election." and inserting in place thereof the following: - If such petition filed as aforesaid is completed by filing with the secretary of the commonwealth not later than ninety days after the law which is the subject of the petition has become law a number of signatures of qualified voters equal in number to not less than one and one half per cent of the entire vote cast for governor at the preceding biennial state election protesting against such law and asking for a referendum thereon, then the secretary of the commonwealth shall submit such law to the people at the next state election, if sixty days intervene between the date when such petition is filed with the secretary of the commonwealth and the date for holding such state election. If sixty days do not so intervene, then it shall be submitted to the people at the next following state election, unless in the meantime it shall have been repealed; and if it shall not be approved by a majority of the qualified voters voting thereon, it shall, at the expiration of thirty days after such election, be thereby repealed; but no such law shall be held to be disapproved if the negative vote is less than thirty per cent of the total number of ballots cast at such state election.

Article LXXXII.

Article LXIV of the Amendments to the Constitution, as amended by Article LXXX of said Amendments, is hereby annulled, and the following is adopted in place thereof:-

Article LXIV. Section 1. The governor, lieutenant-governor, secretary, treasurer and receiver-general, attorney general, and auditor shall be elected quadrennially and councillors, senators and representatives shall be elected biennially. The terms of the governor and lieutenant-governor shall begin at noon on the Thursday next following the first Wednesday in January succeeding their election and shall end at noon on the Thursday next following the first Wednesday in January in the fifth year following their election. If the governor elect shall have died before the qualification of the lieutenant-governor elect, the lieutenant-governor elect upon qualification shall become governor. If both the governor elect and the lieutenant-governor elect shall have died both said offices shall be deemed to be vacant and the provisions of Article LV of the Amendments to the Constitution shall apply. The terms of the secretary, treasurer and receiver-general, attorney general, and auditor shall begin with the third Wednesday in January succeeding their election and shall extend to the third Wednesday in January in the fifth year following their election and until their successors are chosen and qualified. The terms of the councillors shall begin at noon on the Thursday next following the first Wednesday in January succeeding their election and shall end at noon on the Thursday next following the first Wednesday in January in the third year following their election. The terms of senators and representatives shall begin with the first Wednesday in January succeeding their election and shall extend to the first Wednesday in January in the third year following their election and until their successors are chosen and qualified.

Section 2. The general court shall assemble every year on the first Wednesday in January.

Section 3. The first election to which this article shall apply shall be held on the Tuesday next after the first Monday in November in the year nineteen hundred and sixty-six, and thereafter elections for the choice of a governor, lieutenant-governor, secretary, treasurer and receiver-general, attorney general, and auditor shall be held quadrennially on the Tuesday next after the first Monday in November and elections for the choice of councillors, senators and representatives shall be held biennially on the Tuesday next after the first Monday in November.

Article LXXXIII.

The general court shall have full power and authority to provide for prompt and temporary succession to the powers and duties of public offices, of whatever nature and whether filled by election or appointment, the incumbents of which may become unavailable for carrying on the powers and duties of such offices in periods of emergency resulting from disaster caused by enemy attack, and to adopt such other measures as may be necessary and proper for insuring continuity of the government of the commonwealth and the governments of its political subdivisions.

Article LXXXIV.

Article LXII of the Amendments to the Constitution is hereby amended by striking out section 1 and inserting in place thereof the following section: -

Section 1. The commonwealth may give, loan or pledge its credit only by a vote, taken by the yeas and nays, of two-thirds of each house of the general court present and voting thereon. The credit of the commonwealth shall not in any manner be given or loaned to or in aid of any individual, or of any private association, or of any corporation which is privately owned and managed.

Article LXXXV.

Article II of Chapter III of the constitution of the commonwealth is hereby annulled and the following is adopted in place thereof:--

Article II. Each branch of the legislature, as well as the governor or the council, shall have authority to require the opinions of the justices of the supreme judicial court, upon important questions of law, and upon solemn occasions.

Article LXXXVI.

Names of candidates of political parties for the offices of governor and lieutenant-governor shall be grouped on the official ballot for use at state elections according to the parties they represent, and the voter may cast a single vote for any such group, which shall count as a vote for each candidate in such group, but may not cast a vote for only one of the candidates in such group.

Article LXXXVII.

Section 1. For the purpose of transferring, abolishing, consolidating or co-ordinating the whole or any part of any agency, or the functions thereof, within the executive department of the government of the commonwealth, or for the purpose of authorizing any officer of any agency within the executive department of the government of the commonwealth to delegate any of his functions, the governor may prepare one or more reorganization plans, each bearing an identifying number and may present such plan or plans to the general court, together with a message in explanation thereof.

Section 2.

(a) Every such reorganization plan shall be referred to an appropriate committee, to be determined by the Clerks of the Senate and the House of Representatives, with the approval of the President and Speaker, which committee shall not later than thirty days after the date of the Governor's presentation of said plan hold a public hearing thereon and shall not later than ten days after such hearing report that it approves or disapproves such plan and such reorganization plan shall have the force of law upon expiration of the sixty calendar days next following its presentation by the governor to the general court, unless disapproved by a majority vote of the members of either of the two branches of the general court present and voting, the general court not having been prorogued within such sixty days.

(b) After its presentation by the governor to the general court, no such reorganization plan shall be subject to amendment by the general court before expiration of such sixty days.

(c) Any such reorganization plan may provide for its taking effect on any date after expiration of such sixty days and every such reorganization plan shall comply with such conditions as the general court may from time to time prescribe by statute regarding the civil service status, seniority, retirement and other rights of any employee to be affected by such plan.

Article LXXXVIII.

The industrial development of cities and towns is a public function and the commonwealth and the cities and towns therein may provide for the same in such manner as the general court may determine.

Article LXXXIX.

Article II of the Articles of Amendment to the Constitution of the Commonwealth, as amended by Article LXX of said Articles of Amendment, is hereby annulled and the following is dopted in place thereof:

Article II. Section 1. Right of Local Self-Government. - It is the intention of this article to reaffirm the customary and traditional liberties of the people with respect to the conduct of their local government, and to grant and confirm to the people of every city and town the right of self-government in local matters, subject to the provisions of this article and to such standards and requirements as the general court may establish by law in accordance with the provisions of this article.

Section 2. Local Power to adopt, revise or amend Charters. - Any city or town shall have the power to adopt or revise a charter or to amend its existing charter through the procedures set forth in sections three and four. The provisions of any adopted or revised charter or any charter amendment shall not be inconsistent with the constitution or any laws enacted by the general court in conformity with the powers reserved to the general court by section eight.

No town of fewer than twelve thousand inhabitants shall adopt a city form of government, and no town of fewer than six thousand inhabitants shall adopt a form of government providing for a town meeting limited to such inhabitants of the town as may be elected to meet, deliberate, act and vote in the exercise of the corporate powers of the town.

Section 3. Procedure for Adoption or Revision of a Charter by a City or Town. - Every city and town shall have the power to adopt or revise a charter in the following manner: A petition for the adoption or revision of a charter shall be signed by at least fifteen per cent of the number of legal voters residing in such city or town at the preceding state election. Whenever such a petition is filed with the board of registrars of voters of any city or town, the board shall within ten days of its receipt determine the sufficiency and validity of the signatures and certify the results to the city council of the city or board of selectmen of the town, as the case may be. As used in this section, the phrase "board of registrars of voters" shall include any local authority of different designation which performs the duties of such registrars, and the phrase "city council of the city or board of selectmen of the town" shall include local authorities of different designation performing the duties of such council or board. Objections to the sufficiency and validity of the signatures on any such petition as certified by the board of registrars of voters shall be made in the same manner as provided by law for objections to nominations for city or town offices, as the case may be. Within thirty days of receipt of certification of the board of registrars of voters that a petition contains sufficient valid signatures, the city council of the city or board of selectmen of the town shall by order provide for submitting to the voters of the city or town the question of adopting or revising a charter, and for the nomination and election of a charter commission. If the city or town has not previously adopted a charter pursuant to this section, the question submitted to the voters shall be: "Shall a commission be elected to frame a charter for (name of city or town)?" If the city or town has previously adopted a charter pursuant to this section, the question submitted to the voters shall be: "Shall a commission be elected to revise the charter of (name of city or town)?"

The charter commission shall consist of nine voters of the city or town, who shall be elected at large without party or political designation at the city or town election next held at least sixty days after the order of the city council of the city or board of selectmen of the town. The names of candidates for such commission shall be listed alphabetically on the ballot used at such election. Each voter may vote for nine candidates.
The vote on the question submitted and the election of the charter commission shall take place at the same time. If the vote on the question submitted is in the affirmative, the nine

candidates receiving the highest number of votes shall be declared elected.

Within [ten months] after the election of the members of the charter commission, said commission shall submit the charter or revised charter to the city council of the city or the board of selectmen of the town, and such council or board shall provide for publication of the charter and for its submission to the voters of the city or town at the next city or town election held at least two months after such submission by the charter commission. If the charter or revised charter is approved by a majority of the voters of the city or town voting thereon, it shall become effective upon the date fixed in the charter. [See Amendments, Article CXIII]

Section 4. Procedure for Amendment of a Charter by a City or Town. Every city and town shall have the power to amend its charter in the following manner: The legislative body of a city or town may, by a two-thirds vote, propose amendments to the charter of the city or town; provided, that [1] amendments of a city charter may be proposed only with the concurrence of the mayor in every city that has a mayor, and [2] any change in a charter relating in any way to the composition, mode of election or appointment, or terms of office of the legislative body, the mayor or city manager or the board of selectmen or town manager shall be made only by the procedure of charter revision set forth in section three.

All proposed charter amendments shall be published and submitted for approval in the same manner as provided for adoption or revision of a charter.

Section 5. Recording of Charters and Charter Amendments. - Duplicate certificates shall be prepared setting forth any charter that has been adopted or revised and any charter amendments approved, and shall be signed by the city or town clerk. One such certificate shall be deposited in the office of the secretary of the commonwealth and the other shall be recorded in the records of the city or town and deposited among its archives. All courts may take judicial notice of charters and charter amendments of cities and towns.

Section 6. Governmental Powers of Cities and Towns. - Any city or town may, by the adoption, amendment, or repeal of local ordinances or by-laws, exercise any power or function which the general court has power to confer upon it, which is not inconsistent with the constitution or laws enacted by the general court in conformity with powers reserved to the general court in conformity with powers reserved to the general court by section eight, and which is not denied, either expressly or by clear implication, to the city or town by its charter. This section shall apply to every city and town, whether or not it has adopted a charter pursuant to section three.

Section 7. Limitations on Local Powers. - Nothing in this article shall be deemed to grant to any city or town the power to (1) regulate elections other than those prescribed by sections three and four;

(2) to levy, assess and collect taxes;

(3) to borrow money or pledge the credit of the city or town;

(4) to dispose of park land;

(5) to enact private or civil law governing civil relationships except as an incident to an exercise of an independent municipal power; or

(6) to define and provide for the punishment of a felony or to impose imprisonment as a punishment for any violation of law; provided, however, that the foregoing enumerated powers may be granted by the general court in conformity with the constitution and with the powers reserved to the general court by section eight; nor shall the provisions of this article be deemed to diminish the powers of the judicial department of the

commonwealth.

Section 8. Powers of the General Court. - The general court shall have the power to act in relation to cities and towns, but only by general laws which apply alike to all cities or to all towns, or to all cities and towns, or to a class of not fewer than two, and by special laws enacted

(1) on petition filed or approved by the voters of a city or town, or the mayor and city council, or other legislative body, of a city, or the town meeting of a town, with respect to a law relating to that city or town;

(2) by a two-thirds vote of each branch of the general court following a recommendation by the governor;

(3) to erect and constitute metropolitan or regional entities, embracing any two or more cities or towns or cities and towns, or established with other than existing city or town boundaries, for any general or special public purpose or purposes, and to grant to these entities such powers, privileges and immunities as the general court shall deem necessary or expedient for the regulation and government thereof; or

(4) solely for the incorporation or dissolution of cities or towns as corporate entities, alteration of city or town boundaries, and merger or consolidation of cities and towns, or any of these matters.

Subject to the foregoing requirements, the general court may provide optional plans of city or town organization and government under which an optional plan may be adopted or abandoned by majority vote of the voters of the city or town voting thereon at a city or town election; provided, that no town of fewer than twelve thousand inhabitants may be authorized to adopt a city form of government, and no town of fewer than six thousand inhabitants may be authorized to adopt a form of town government providing for town meeting limited to such inhabitants of the town as may be elected to meet, deliberate, act and vote in the exercise of the corporate powers of the town. This section shall apply to every city and town whether or not it has adopted a charter pursuant to section three.

Section 9. Existing Special Laws. - All special laws relating to individual cities or towns shall remain in effect and have the force of an existing city or town charter, but shall be subject to amendment or repeal through the adoption, revision or amendment of a charter by a city or town in accordance with the provisions of sections three and four and shall be subject to amendment or repeal by laws enacted by the general court in conformity with the powers reserved to the general court by section eight.

Article XC.

Section 1. Article II of section I of Chapter I of Part the Second of the constitution is hereby amended by striking out the second paragraph and inserting in place thereof the following paragraph:-

And in order to prevent unnecessary delays, if any bill or resolve shall not be returned by the governor within ten days after it shall have been presented, the same shall have the force of a law.

Section 2. Article I of the Articles of Amendment to the Constitution is hereby annulled and the following is adopted in place thereof:--

Article I. If any bill or resolve shall be objected to, and not approved by the governor, and if the general court shall adjourn within ten days after the same shall have been laid before the governor for his approbation, and thereby prevent his returning it with his objections, as provided by the constitution, such bill or resolve shall not become a law, nor have force as such.

Section 3. Article LVI of the Articles of the Articles of Amendments to the Constitution is hereby annulled and the following is adopted in place thereof:--

Article LVI The governor, within ten days after any bill or resolve shall have been laid before him, shall have the right to return it to the branch of the general court in which it originated with a recommendation that any amendment or amendments specified by him be made therein. Such bill or resolve shall thereupon be before the general court and subject to amendment and re-enactment. If such bill or resolve is re-enacted in any form it shall again be laid before the governor for his action, but he shall have no right to return the same a second time with a recommendation to amend.

Section 4. Article LXIII of the Articles of Amendment to the Constitution is hereby amended by striking out Section 5 and inserting in place thereof the following section:--

Section 5. Submission to the Governor. - The governor may disapprove or reduce items or parts of items in any bill appropriating money. So much of such bill as he approves shall upon his signing the same become law. As to each item disapproved or reduced he shall transmit to the house in which the bill originated his reason for such disapproval or reduction, and the procedure shall then be the same as in the case of a bill disapproved as a whole. In case he shall fail so to transmit his reasons for such disapproval or reduction within ten days after the bill shall have been presented to him, such items shall have the force of law unless the general court by adjournment shall prevent such transmission, in which case they shall not be law.

Article XCI.

Whenever the governor transmits to the president of the senate and the speaker of the house his written declaration that he is unable to discharge the powers and duties of his office, the office of governor shall be deemed to be vacant within the meaning of this Constitution.

Whenever the chief justice and a majority of the associate justices of the supreme judicial court, or such other body as the general court may by law provide, transmit to the president of the senate and the speaker of the house their written declaration that the governor is unable to discharge the powers and duties of his office, the office of governor shall be deemed to be vacant within the meaning of this Constitution.

Thereafter, in either of the above cases, whenever the governor transmits to the president of the senate and the speaker of the house his written declaration that no inability exists such vacancy shall be deemed to have terminated four days thereafter and the governor shall resume the powers and duties of his office unless the chief justice and a majority of the associate justices of the supreme judicial court, or such other body as the general court may by law provide, transmit within said four days to the president of the senate and the speaker of the house their written declaration that the governor is unable to discharge the powers and duties of his office. Thereupon the general court shall decide the issue, assembling within forty-eight hours for that purpose if not in session. If the general court within twenty-one days after receipt of the latter written declaration, or, if the general court is not in session, within twenty-one days after the general court is required to assemble, determine by a vote, taken by yeas and nays, of two thirds of each house present and voting thereon, that the governor is unable to discharge the powers and duties of his office, the office of governor shall continue to be deemed to be vacant; otherwise such vacancy shall be deemed to have terminated and the governor shall resume the powers and duties of his office.

If a vacancy in the office of governor, as described in this Article, continues for six months and if such six-month period expires more than five months prior to a biennial state election other than an election for governor, there shall be an election of governor at such biennial state election for the balance of the unexpired four-year term.

If a vacancy in the office of governor, as described in this Article, continues for six months and if such six-month period expires more than five months prior to a biennial state election other than an election for governor, there shall be an election of governor at such biennial state election for the balance of the unexpired four-year term.

Article XCII.

Section 1. In the year nineteen hundred and seventy-one and every tenth year thereafter a census of the inhabitants of each city and town shall be taken. Said census shall specify the number of inhabitants residing in each precinct of each town and in each precinct and ward of each city. Said census shall be the basis for determining the representative districts for the ten year period beginning with the first Wednesday in the fourth January following the taking of said census; provided that such districts as established in the year nineteen hundred and sixty-eight shall continue until the first Wednesday in January in the year nineteen hundred and seventy-five.

The house of representatives shall consist of two hundred and forty members. The general court shall, at its first regular session after the year in which said census was taken, divide the commonwealth into two hundred and forty representative districts of contiguous territory so that each representative will represent an equal number of inhabitants, as nearly as may be; and such districts shall be formed, as nearly as may be, without uniting two counties or parts of two or more counties, two towns or parts of two or more towns, two cities or parts of two or more cities, or a city and a town, or parts of cities and towns, into one district; provided, however, that the county of Dukes county and Nantucket county shall each be a representative district. Such districts shall also be so formed that no town containing less than six thousand inhabitants according to said census shall be divided. The general court may by law limit the time within which judicial proceedings may be instituted calling in question any such division. Every representative, for one year at least immediately preceding his election, shall have been an inhabitant of the district for which he is chosen, and shall cease to represent such district when he shall cease to be an inhabitant of the commonwealth. The manner of calling and conducting the elections for the choice of representatives, and of ascertaining their election, shall be prescribed by law.

Section 2. Each census of inhabitants required in section one shall likewise be the basis for determining the senatorial districts and also the councillor districts for the ten year period beginning with the first Wednesday in the fourth January following the taking of such census; provided that such districts as established prior to the year nineteen hundred and seventy-one shall continue until the first Wednesday in January in the year nineteen hundred and seventy-five. The senate shall consist of forty members. The general court shall, at its first regular session after the year in which said census is taken, divide the commonwealth into forty districts of contiguous territory, each district to contain, as nearly as may be, an equal number of inhabitants according to said census; and such districts shall be formed, as nearly as may be, without uniting two counties, or parts of two or more counties into one district. The general court may by law limit the time within which judicial proceedings may be instituted calling in question such division. Each district shall elect one senator, who shall have been an inhabitant of this commonwealth five years at least immediately preceding his election, and at the time of his election shall be an inhabitant of the district for which he is chosen; and he shall cease to represent such senatorial district when he shall cease to be an inhabitant of the commonwealth.

Section 3. Articles XXI and XXII of the Amendments to the Constitution, as appearing in Article LXXI of said Amendments, are hereby annulled.] [Annulled by Amendments, Article CI]

Article XCIII.

Article III of the Amendments to the Constitution, as amended, is hereby further amended by striking out the words "within the commonwealth one year, and".

Article XCIV.

Article III of the amendments to the Constitution, as amended, is hereby further amended by striking out the word "twenty-one" and inserting in place thereof the word: -- nineteen.

Article XCV.

Article III of the Amendments to the Constitution, as amended, is hereby further amended by striking out the words "pauper and".

Article XCVI.

The general court shall have power to authorize the commonwealth to make loans, on such terms as it may deem reasonable, to any residents of the commonwealth for tuition and board at any college, university or other institution of higher learning.

Article XCVII.

Article XLIX of the Amendments to the Constitution is hereby annulled and the following is adopted in place thereof: - The people shall have the right to clean air and water, freedom from excessive and unnecessary noise, and the natural, scenic, historic, and esthetic qualities of their environment; and the protection of the people in their right to the conservation, development and utilization of the agricultural, mineral, forest, water, air and other natural resources is hereby declared to be a public purpose.

The general court shall have the power to enact legislation necessary or expedient to protect such rights.

In the furtherance of the foregoing powers, the general court shall have the power to provide for the taking, upon payment of just compensation therefor, or for the acquisition by purchase or otherwise, of lands and easements or such other interests therein as may be deemed necessary to accomplish these purposes.

Lands and easements taken or acquired for such purposes shall not be used for other purposes or otherwise disposed of except by laws enacted by a two thirds vote, taken by yeas and nays, of each branch of the general court.

Article XCVIII.

Article I of Chapter III of Part the Second of the Constitution, as amended by Article LVIII of the Amendments to the Constitution, is hereby annulled and the following Article is adopted in place thereof:-

Article I. The tenure, that all commissioned officers shall by law have in their offices, shall be expressed in their respective commissions. All judicial officers, duly appointed, commissioned and sworn, shall hold their offices during good behavior, excepting such concerning whom there is different provision made in this Constitution; provided, nevertheless, the governor, with the consent of the council, may remove them upon the address of both houses of the legislature; and provided, also, that the governor, with the consent of the council, may after due notice and hearing retire them because of advanced age or mental or physical disability; and provided further, that upon attaining seventy years of age said judges shall be retired. Such retirement shall be subject to any provisions made by law as to pensions or allowances payable to such officers upon their voluntary retirement.

Article XCIX.

Full power and authority are hereby given and granted to the general court to prescribe, for the purpose of developing and conserving agricultural or horticultural lands, that such lands shall be valued, for the purpose of taxation, according to their agricultural or horticultural uses; provided, however, that no parcel of land which is less than five acres in area or which has not been actively devoted to agricultural or horticultural uses for the two years preceding the tax year shall be valued at less than fair market value under this article.

Article C.

Article III of the Amendments to the Constitution, as amended, is hereby further amended by striking out the word indicating the age at which a citizen shall have a right to vote in an election of Governor and other public officers and inserting in place thereof the following word: -- eighteen.

Article CI.

Section 1. In the year nineteen hundred and seventy-five and every tenth year thereafter a census of the inhabitants of each city and town shall be taken. Said census shall specify the number of inhabitants residing in each precinct of each town and in each precinct and ward of each city. Said census shall be the basis for determining the representative districts for the ten year period beginning with the first Wednesday in the fourth January following the taking of said census; provided that such districts as established based on the census in the year nineteen hundred and seventy-one shall terminate on the first Wednesday in January in the year nineteen hundred and seventy-nine.] [See Amendments, Articles CIX and CXVII]

The House of Representatives shall consist of one hundred and sixty members. The General Court shall, at its first regular session after the year in which said census was taken, divide the Commonwealth into one hundred and sixty representative districts of contiguous territory so that each representative will represent an equal number of inhabitants, as nearly as may be; and such districts shall be formed, as nearly as may be, without uniting two counties or parts of two or more counties, two towns or parts of two or more towns, two cities or parts of two or more cities, or a city and a town, or parts of cities and towns, into one district. Such districts shall also be so formed that no town containing less than twenty-five hundred inhabitants according to said census shall be divided. The General Court may by law limit the time within which judicial proceedings may be instituted calling in question any such division. Every representative, for one year at least immediately preceding his election, shall have been an inhabitant of the district for which he is chosen and shall cease to represent such district when he shall cease to be an inhabitant of the Commonwealth. The manner of calling and conducting the elections for the choice of representatives, and of ascertaining their election, shall be prescribed by law.
Section 2. [Each such census of inhabitants required in section one shall likewise be the basis for determining the senatorial

districts and also the councillor districts for the ten year period beginning with the first Wednesday in the fourth January following the taking of such census; provided that such districts as established based on the census in the year nineteen hundred and seventy-one shall terminate on the first Wednesday in January in the year nineteen hundred and seventy-nine.] The Senate shall consist of forty members. The General Court shall, at its first regular session after the year in which said census is taken, divide the Commonwealth into forty districts of contiguous territory, each district to contain, as nearly as may be, an equal number of inhabitants according to said census; and such districts shall be formed, as nearly as may be, without uniting two counties, or parts of two or more counties, into one district. The General Court may by law limit the time within which judicial proceedings may be instituted calling in question such division. Each district shall elect one senator, who shall have been an inhabitant of this Commonwealth five years at least immediately preceding his election and at the time of his election shall be an inhabitant of the district for which he is chosen; and he shall cease to represent such senatorial district when he shall cease to be an inhabitant of the Commonwealth. The manner of calling and conducting the elections for the choice of senators and councillors, and of ascertaining their election, shall be prescribed by law.

Section 3. Original jurisdiction is hereby vested in the supreme judicial court upon the petition of any voter of the Commonwealth, filed with the clerk of the supreme judicial court for the Commonwealth, for judicial relief relative to the establishment of House of Representatives, councillor and senatorial districts.

Section 4. Article XCII of the Amendments to the Constitution is hereby annulled.

Article CII.

Article LII of the Articles of Amendment to the Constitution is hereby annulled and the following is adopted in place thereof:- Article LII. The General Court, by concurrent vote of the two houses, may take a recess or recesses amounting to not more than thirty days.

Article CIII.

Article XLVI of the Articles of Amendment to the Constitution of the Commonwealth is hereby amended by striking out section 2 and inserting in place thereof the following section:-
Section 2. No grant, appropriation or use of public money or property or loan of credit shall be made or authorized by the Commonwealth or any political subdivision thereof for the purpose of founding, maintaining or aiding any infirmary, hospital, institution, primary or secondary school, or charitable or religious undertaking which is not publicly owned and under the exclusive control, order and supervision of public officers or public agents authorized by the Commonwealth or federal authority or both, except that appropriations may be made for the maintenance and support of the Soldiers' Home in Massachusetts and for free public libraries in any city or town and to carry out legal obligations, if any, already entered into; and no such grant, appropriation or use of public money or property or loan of public credit shall be made or authorized for the purpose of founding, maintaining or aiding any church, religious denomination or society. Nothing herein contained shall be construed to prevent the Commonwealth from making grants-in-aid to private higher educational institutions or to students or parents or guardians of students attending such institutions.

Article CIV.

Article LXXVIII of the Amendments to the Constitution is hereby annulled and the following is adopted in place thereof:-
Article LXXVIII. No revenue from fees, duties, excises or license taxes relating to registration, operation or use of vehicle on public highways, or to fuels used for propelling such vehicles, shall be expended for other than cost of administration of laws providing for such revenue, making of refunds and adjustments in relation thereto, payment of highway obligations, or cost of construction, reconstruction, maintenance and repair of public highways and bridges, and mass transportation lines and of the enforcement of state traffic laws, and for other mass transportation purposes; and such revenue shall be expended by the commonwealth or its counties, cities and towns for said highway and mass transportation purposes only and in such manner as the general court may direct; provided, that this amendment shall not apply to revenue from any excise tax imposed in lieu of local property taxes for the privilege of registering such vehicles.

Article CV.

Article XLV of the articles of amendment to the constitution, as amended by Article LXXVI of said articles of amendment, is hereby annulled and the following is adopted in place thereof:-
Article XLV. The general court shall have power to provide by law for voting, in the choice of any officer to be elected or upon any question submitted at an election, by qualified voters of the commonwealth who, at the time of such an election, are absent from the city or town of which they are inhabitants or are unable by reason of physical disability to cast their votes in person at the polling places or who hold religious beliefs in conflict with the act of voting on the day on which such an election is to be held.

Article CVI.

Article I of Part the First of the Constitution is hereby annulled and the following is adopted:-

All people are born free and equal and have certain natural, essential and unalienable rights; among which may be reckoned the right of enjoying and defending their lives and liberties; that of acquiring, possessing and protecting property; in fine, that of seeking and obtaining their safety and happiness. Equality under the law shall not be denied or abridged because of sex, race, color, creed or national origin.

Article CVII.

Section 2 of Article LXIII of the Articles of Amendment to the Constitution of the Commonwealth is hereby annulled and the following is adopted in place thereof:-

Section 2. The Budget. - Within three weeks after the convening of the general court the governor shall recommend to the general court a budget which shall contain a statement of all proposed expenditures of the commonwealth for the fiscal year, including those already authorized by law, and of all taxes, revenues, loans and other means by which such expenditures shall be defrayed. In the first year of the term of office of a governor who has not served in the preceding year said governor shall recommend such budget within eight weeks after the convening of the general court. The budget shall be arranged in such form as the general court may by law prescribe, or, in default thereof, as the governor shall determine. For the purpose of preparing his budget, the governor shall have the power to require any board, commission, officer or department to furnish him with any information which he may deem necessary.

Article CVIII.

Article XLVIII of the Amendments to the Constitution of the Commonwealth is hereby amended by striking out, under the heading "GENERAL PROVISION", all of subheading "IV. Information for Voters.", as amended by section 4 of Article LXXIV of said Amendments, and inserting in place thereof the following subheading:

IV. Information for Voters.

The secretary of the commonwealth shall cause to be printed and sent to each person eligible to vote in the commonwealth or to each residence of one or more persons eligible to vote in the commonwealth the full text of every measure to be submitted to the people, together with a copy of the legislative committee's majority reports, if there be such, with the names of the majority and minority members thereon, a statement of the votes of the general court on the measure, and a fair, concise summary of the measure as such summary will appear on the ballot; and shall, in such manner as may be provided by law, cause to be prepared and sent other information and arguments for and against the measure.

Article CIX.

The first paragraph of Section 1 oF Article CI of the Amendments to the Constitution of the Commonwealth is hereby amended by striking out the second sentence and inserting in place thereof the following two sentences:-

For purposes of said census every person shall be considered an inhabitant of the city or town of his usual place of residence in accordance with standards used by the United States from time to time in conducting the federal census required by Section 2 of Article I of the Constitution of the United States subject to such exceptions as the general court may provide by law. Said census shall specify the number of inhabitants of each precinct of each town and of each precinct and ward of each city.

Article CX.

Article XLI of the Amendments to the Constitution is hereby annulled and the following Article is adopted in place thereof:- Full power and authority are hereby given and granted to the general court to prescribe for wild or forest lands retained in a natural state for the preservation of wildlife and other natural resources and lands for recreational uses, such methods of taxation as will develop and conserve the forest resources, wildlife and other natural resources and the environmental benefits of recreational lands within the commonwealth.

Article CXI.

No student shall be assigned to or denied admittance to a public school on the basis of race, color, national origin or creed.

Article CXII.

Article IV of chapter 1 of Part the Second of the Constitution is hereby amended by inserting after the words "and to impose and levy proportional and reasonable assessments, rates and taxes, upon all the inhabitants of, and persons resident, and estates lying, within said Commonwealth" the words: -, except that, in addition to the powers conferred under Articles XLI and XCIX of the Amendments, the general court may classify real property according to its use in no more than four classes and to assess, rate and tax such property differently in the classes so established, but proportionately in the same class, and except that reasonable exemptions may be granted.

Article CXIII.

The first sentence of the sixth paragraph of Section 3 of Article II of the Amendments to the Constitution of the Commonwealth, as appearing in Article LXXXIX of said Amendments, is hereby amended by striking out the words "ten months" and inserting in place thereof the words: -- eighteen months.

Article CXIV.

No otherwise qualified handicapped individual shall, solely by reason of his handicap, be excluded from the participation in, denied the benefits of, or be subject to discrimination under any program or activity within the commonwealth.

Article CXV.

No law imposing additional costs upon two or more cities or towns by the regulation of the compensation, hours, status, conditions or benefits of municipal employment shall be effective in any city or town until such law is accepted by vote or by the appropriation of money for such purposes, in the case of a city, by the city council in accordance with its charter, and in the case of a town, by a town meeting or town council, unless such law has been enacted by a two-thirds vote of each house of the general court present and voting thereon, or unless the general court, at the same session in which such law is enacted, has provided for the assumption by the commonwealth of such additional cost.

Article CXVI.

Article XXVI of part 1 of the Constitution of the Commonwealth is hereby amended by adding the following two sentences: No provision of the Constitution, however, shall be construed as prohibiting the imposition of the punishment of death. The general court may, for the purpose of protecting the general welfare of the citizens, authorize the imposition of the punishment of death by the courts of law having jurisdiction of crimes subject to the punishment of death.

Article CXVII.

Section 1. Section 1 of Article CI of the Articles of Amendment to the Constitution is hereby amended by striking out the first paragraph, as amended by Article CIX of said Articles of Amendment, and inserting in place thereof the following paragraph: - The federal census shall be the basis for determining the representative districts for the ten year period beginning with the first Wednesday in the [fifth] January following the taking of said census. [Amended by Amendments, Article CXIX, sect. 1]

Section 2. Section 2 of said Article CI of said Articles of Amendment is hereby amended by striking out the first sentence and inserting in place thereof the following sentence: - Said federal census shall likewise be the basis for determining the senatorial districts and also the councillor districts for the ten year period beginning with the first Wednesday in the [fifth] January following the taking of such census. [Amended by Amendments, Article CXIX, sect. 2]

Article CXVIII.

The base compensation as of January first, nineteen hundred and ninety-six, of members of the general court shall not be changed except as provided in this article. As of the first Wednesday in January of the year two thousand and one and every second year thereafter, such base compensation shall be increased or decreased at the same rate as increases or decreases in the median household income for the commonwealth for the preceding two year period, as ascertained by the governor.

Article CXIX.

Section 1. Section 1 of Article CI of the Articles of Amendment to the Constitution is hereby amended by striking out the first paragraph, as appearing in section 1 of CXVII of said Articles of Amendment, and inserting in place thereof the following paragraph:--

The federal census shall be the basis for determining the representative districts for the ten year period beginning with the first Wednesday in the third January following the taking of said census.

Section 2. Section 2 of said Article CI is hereby amended by striking out the first sentence, as appearing in section 2 of said Article CXVII, and inserting in place thereof the following sentence:-- Said federal census shall likewise be the basis for determining the senatorial districts and also the councillor districts for the ten year period beginning with the first Wednesday in the third January following the taking of said census.

Article CXX.

Article III of the Amendments to the Constitution, as amended, is hereby further amended by inserting after the word "upwards" the following words:-- , excepting persons who are incarcerated in a correctional facility due to a felony conviction, and.

www.ingramcontent.com/pod-product-compliance
Lightning Source LLC
Chambersburg PA
CBHW052243220526
45471CB00001B/174